Praise for
Write Yourself Into Your Dreams

"An unconventional and ultimately uplifting call to reclaim your own life story."

—*KIRKUS REVIEWS*

"There are incredible riches in this method that are beyond what you can even begin to imagine."

—WENDY L. ROGERS, PH.D., PSYCHOLOGIST

"It's like *The Artist's Way* meets *The Secret.*"

—JANA KELLAM, BESTSELLING AUTHOR

"Within two weeks of starting the process (and after not working for three years), I got a call to be in the writers' room of a popular TV series."

—JULIE L., WRITER

"I feel 15 years younger and like anything is possible. This method is astounding."

—DAVID DORN, ACTOR AND MODEL

Write Yourself Into Your Dreams

WRITE YOURSELF INTO YOUR *Dreams*

with the Essential Life Story Method

Teri Wade

TEA HOUSE PRESS

Disclaimer:

The resources made available in this book are not a
substitute for the advice of a physician or mental health
care professional. Teri Wade and The Evolving Artist, LLC
cannot be held responsible for the use of the information
provided. The reader should seek help from a trained
professional as needed when making personal healthcare
decisions or decisions regarding the healthcare of others.

Acknowledgements

My heartfelt thanks to all of my clients and friends who've contributed to the creation of this book over the past ten years. I also want to thank Ty Hammond, Jim Dodds, and Ashley Williams for your feedback and edits at earlier stages of the process. Thank you, David MacDonald, for coming along at the right time and helping me relax into my feminine energy, which was so necessary for completing this book. Thank you, Jessica Leventhal, for your patience, kindness, brilliance, and thorough edits—I loved growing closer to you through this journey. And thank you, Jana Kellam, for exploring every sentence of this book with me and midwifing it into a version that I could actually release to the world. Your love, kindness, genius, and friendship mean the world to me, and I couldn't have done it without you.

Thank you, Mom and Dad, for supporting me in Spirit every day. Thank you, Jim Wade and Kelly Reed, for always being there. Thank you, my wonderful daughters, Aurelia and Phoenix, for being wise beyond your years and bringing so much love, joy and inspiration into my life. Thank you, Arutem, the spirit of the Amazon rainforest, and the Achuar people for inspiring me to write this book. You taught me the true value of dreams and provided me with a visceral experience of what peace and daily connection to Spirit feels like, so that it could begin to become the story of my life, and God-willing, the story of us all.

Contents

Chapter 6: Identifying Your Story Core 96

Chapter 7: Turning Your Greatest Current
Challenge into a Magical New Reality 107

Chapter 8: Discovering Your Greatest Dreams 119

Chapter 9: Assembling Your ELS 131

Chapter 10: Mastering Your Messages 144

Chapter 11: Weaving and Balancing Your ELS 159

Words are, in my not-so-humble opinion,
our most inexhaustible form of magic.

—ALBUS DUMBLEDORE

Once Upon a Time...

There was a little girl whose parents were cursed by a powerful spell. They couldn't see their own goodness, nor hers, and so they told the little girl so many bad things about herself from the day she was born that she started to believe that the bad things were true.

The little girl became plagued by voices that fought in her mind. One voice said, "Oh, I'd love to be a writer one day." And another argued, "You can't do that... who do you think you are?" This internal battle went on for so long that she wasn't even aware it was happening. And even if she had been conscious of the war in her mind, she would have had no idea how to make peace.

Then one day, the little girl's fairy godmother sent her a message. "Oh, my dear one," she said, "what you long for is actually meant to be yours. The reason for your struggle is simply this: you've grown imprisoned by the walls of a story that makes you feel small, unworthy, and weak. But I will teach you the magic to write your story anew, for when you do, there will be no force in the world that can keep your dreams from you."

Preface

In 2009, I was feeling stuck trying to finish a novel I'd been working on for years, about a humanoid rabbit who expands consciousness by traveling through time and space. I felt like I lacked some essential knowledge about story structure, so I picked up a copy of Joseph Campbell's *The Hero with a Thousand Faces* with the hope it could help me. As I read about the phases of a hero's journey, I tried to see the main character of my novel through the lens Campbell provides; but the more I read, the more I saw my *own* journey—particularly a journey I had made, eight years prior, to the Amazon rainforest, where I lived with an indigenous tribe.

Campbell describes the primary stages of a hero's journey, which include being called to an important quest, answering that call, crossing the threshold into a new world, and being tested in ways that yield new wisdom. While each step of the hero's journey contains challenges, Campbell says that the most difficult step—so difficult in fact, that most heroes never take it—is the final one: returning home and sharing what they've learned with their own people.

When I lived in the Amazon, I was the happiest I'd ever been, and I cried from joy every day. But for years after returning home, I struggled with constant low-level anxiety. My journey had been so otherworldly and enlightening, yet I had no idea what to *do* with what I'd learned; I had no idea how to integrate what I'd experienced in the Amazon into my life back home. While *The Hero with a Thousand Faces* didn't provide me with a road map for *how* to take this last crucial step of my own hero's journey, it planted an important seed. I finally knew what I needed to do and why I wasn't at peace when it came to the Amazon: my journey was incomplete. I still needed to share what I'd learned with people in my own culture.

A few months later, I was daydreaming about publishing my first book—something I'd wanted to do since I was seven years old. I noticed that no matter how hard I tried, my mind wouldn't let me stay with the dream for more than a few moments. It kept showing me scenes from my childhood, when my father physically and emotionally abused me. It was as if my mind was trying to pull me back into "reality" by saying, *That's a nice story, Teri, that you want to be an author and help people, but look at what has happened in your past. People like you don't get to have what you're dreaming of.*

Just like the little girl in the fairy tale at the beginning of this book, I realized that I had two competing stories in my mind. There was the story of my dreams coming true, which felt nice, but had little basis in reality. And there was the story of my abusive childhood, which felt heavy and all too real. It felt like the story of my past was beating the crap out of the story of my dreams. But then I thought of another way of looking at it: my two stories were sitting on opposite sides of the Grand Canyon, with no bridge between them. Unlike the little girl, I didn't have a fairy godmother to tell me how to get from one story to the other.

So I asked myself, *What if I could build a bridge?*

My favorite thing to do while earning my history degree from U.C. Berkeley was to come up with a new theory about a past event or time period—a theory that, if true, could change how people relate to the present—and then dive into the research to prove my thesis was true. I had an epiphany that maybe I could write a new version of my own story, as if it were a history assignment, where my thesis was that my dreams were actually meant to come true. I didn't know what that new version of my story would look like yet, but I knew—as a student of history—that it could be written.

My next thought was that surely there must be a book out there that could teach me how to do it—how to recreate my story in a way that would set me free. But I read every book I could find on the subject of writing your story and was surprised to find that the one I needed didn't exist.

I read books that tried to convince me that my story had value, books about how I didn't need to be famous to write it, and books that provided writing prompts and memory-jogging tools. But none of the books I read provided a method, or a process, for writing my story from beginning to end. More importantly, none of them even broached the idea that I could *change my future* by finding new ways of telling the story of my past. The overwhelming majority were simply written for older people to record their stories before they died.

All of the books I read about writing your story had three things in common that didn't work for me. First, they were focused on the past for its own sake; and I needed a book that focused on the past for the purpose of altering the future. Second, they assumed that history was static; and I needed a book that understood that history is inherently fluid and alterable. Third, all of the books I read were about writing a memoir—a long-form personal history; and I intuitively felt that I would get lost in the labyrinth of such a long story. In order to actually *see* the areas of my story that needed to evolve, and to then evolve them, I needed to write a *short* story.

I thought, *Maybe I'm supposed to write that book... maybe other people need what I'm looking for, too.*

I was a busy stay-at-home mom with two baby girls at the time, so the thought came and went. Then, several months later, my life fell apart at the seams, and the time opened up. I went through a contentious divorce, after which I was with my children only half the time. Suddenly I was on my own every other week, struggling to make ends meet.

One night I was sitting alone, feeling powerless and sorry for myself: I didn't have money to buy food and I couldn't even go to my parents for help because they had both died in the previous two years. To top it all off, I felt like a fraud. I thought, *I've been successfully helping people change their lives for over a decade, but how can I promote my work and build up my business when I'm in such a terrible place myself? And how did I even get to such a terrible place to begin with?*

I thought about the realization I'd had while reading *The Hero with a Thousand Faces*. I thought about the epiphany I'd had while daydreaming about publishing my book. I thought about my time in the Amazon rainforest and how I cried every day from happiness. And I wondered, *Why haven't I been able to feel as happy here as I felt there?* And then, I thought that maybe writing my story in a way that integrated my Amazon experience would help me feel that same level of peace and joy here at home. Perhaps it was time to finally rewrite my history and prove my thesis, that I could have all of the things I was yearning for: greater daily happiness, a renewed connection with the Amazon rainforest, a successful business doing what I love, a fulfilling romantic partnership, a peaceful co-parenting dynamic with my ex, and a published book that truly helps people.

In a moment of urgency, that felt a lot like the powerful surges I had experienced while giving birth, I got off the couch and rushed to find a pen. My story poured out of me, like it had always been right there, under the surface, and I had so many breakthroughs right from the start.

One breakthrough was that I had a lifelong pattern of ignoring my intuition when it came to men. I'd always been so afraid of being alone that time and again I argued myself out of seeing red flags for what they were. There wasn't some big, complicated reason my marriage had ended so terribly. It was pretty simple: I hadn't listened to my gut.

Another insight I gained was that I had a lifelong pattern of blaming myself for things that weren't my fault, a pattern that clearly stemmed from my alcoholic father having also blamed me for things that weren't my fault. I could see how this same pattern had repeated itself throughout most of my romantic relationships, as well. It suddenly made sense that a life built on such unhealthy foundational patterns *had* to crumble to the ground to give me space to build a new, more loving and healthy foundation for myself.

The realizations I had while writing my story that night were significant, but they were just the beginning. Rewriting the *short* version of my life story became an obsession. I was often up at all hours of the night, like a mad scientist, upgrading my own story and simultaneously developing the Essential Life Story Process—which I will lead you through in this book—so that you could easily replicate and benefit from everything I was learning through trial and error.

The answer to the question of whether it was possible to build a bridge between the story of my past and the story of my dreams coming true was a resounding *YES!* Sometimes, as I made breakthroughs in my written story, I felt watery inside, as if my body was letting go of old parts of my story that I no longer needed. I felt new channels of possibility open between me and my dreams… channels that didn't previously exist. And then, like magic, those dreams came true.

All the significant dreams that I've manifested through the process of recreating my story were planted into my narrative before they came to life. The ELS Method empowered me to return to the Amazon rainforest for the first time in fifteen years, grow a successful business doing what I love, have my first healthy romantic relationship, create a peaceful co-parenting dynamic with my ex, and publish this book. Perhaps even more important than those obvious, tangible changes are the more subtle, intangible shifts that the ELS Method brought me: I often cry tears of joy *here* now, like I used to do in the jungle; I feel at peace inside of my own mind; I feel a deep, daily connection to Spirit; and I feel like my own best friend, instead of my own worst enemy.

Many people have tried to tell me that there aren't enough people out there who are willing to do the work to warrant the publication of this book. But the constant drive I've felt over the past ten years to put this book in your hands tells me otherwise. I believe that you, and others like you, were calling it forth, through me, all along.

The Essential Life Story journey that you're about to embark on will empower you to discover deeper meaning in your life; believe and achieve what used to feel impossible; and create your own fate with the power of pen and paper—no matter what has happened in your past. I am honored to be your guide through this process and to help you transform the story of your life into the uniquely healing, empowering, and inspiring force of nature that it's meant to be.

Write Yourself Into Your Dreams

Introduction

This is not a how-to book about writing your memoir, and it's not even a book about writing a story for other people to read. This is a book about writing a *short* story (about five pages long) for *yourself*—a story that changes your life in magical ways.

To explain how changing your story can change your life so dramatically, I'd like to begin with a metaphor. In the cult-classic film, *Donnie Darko*, a teenage boy named Donnie is given a book from his teacher called *The Philosophy of Time Travel*, which describes how every person travels through time and space along a channel, or continuum, that emanates from inside of them. Soon after reading the book, Donnie actually *sees* what the book describes. He watches a flowing energetic channel emerge from his chest, and then feels compelled to follow it. Shortly after that experience, Donnie talks to his teacher about these continuums, and his teacher says that the trajectory of each person's continuum can change at any time based upon the decisions they make in the moment.

While there is a lot of debate about what actually happens in *Donnie Darko* and what it all means, I believe it resonated so deeply with so many people because it provides a visual explanation for a phenomenon that we're each experiencing every day, without even knowing it. We're each traveling along a continuum that emanates from inside of us, one that stretches into a future that is predetermined by the continuum itself.

Donnie's teacher says that the choices you make in each moment determine the trajectory of your continuum, but I believe that your continuum is determined by something much deeper: the story of your life... a story that dictates not only your choices, but your every thought, feeling, and action.

The story of your life is an unconscious narrative you carry inside that permeates every cell of your being and determines what is possible for you. The energy of your story radiates outward, producing a field that attracts everything matching its frequency—good or bad. Your story also projects the continuum you travel along through time and space, which leads to an ending that perfectly matches the current version of the story you're carrying. With the right tools and understanding, you can gain access to your unconscious narrative and transform it in deep and authentic ways that immediately change both the path you follow through life and your ultimate destination.

I know it may sound like something out of a sci-fi film—the idea that you can change your story in writing and have it immediately change your life—but I assure you, it's real. I don't want you to take my word for it, though. I wrote this book so that you can experience the truth of what I'm describing for yourself, first-hand.

What Is Your Essential Life Story?

Your Essential Life Story (ELS) is a 5-page narrative that changes what you believe is possible and brings your Greatest Dreams to life—no matter who you are and no matter what has happened in your past. You also don't have to know what your dreams *are* right now to experience these results, because the ELS Method will *reveal* your Greatest Dreams to you. You'll craft your ELS in 12 steps—each building upon the last. I poured thousands of hours into optimizing the ELS Method to ensure that you are empowered with the structure, exercises, and guidance you need to successfully transform your story into one that forever changes you.

When you read your completed ELS in the future, you'll feel at peace and empowered by your past and easily see how your past perfectly prepared you to realize your dreams. You'll believe that your dreams, which will be woven into the fabric of your new story, will certainly come true and in greater ways than you could ever imagine.

Once crafted, your ELS will automatically replace your old, unconscious narrative, and become the new story that you carry inside, the new director of your continuum, the new lens through which you see the world, and the new source of your daily thoughts, feelings, and actions that determine your reality. No longer will you have to struggle to convince yourself that you can be, do, or have what you want. You will be able to enjoy your new trajectory in life, manifest your dreams with greater ease than ever before, and finally feel like the hero of your own story.

The Pervasive Problem of Story-Blindness

As a human, you relate to your story in much the same way that a fish relates to water—you're so immersed in it that you don't even know it exists. Here's an example from popular culture that illustrates how blind we are to our stories. Think for a moment about how many times you've heard someone say, "That's the story of my life…" followed by something bad that they wish would stop happening.

"That's the story of my life—I'm a day late and a dollar short."

"That's the story of my life—they always turn out to be jerks."

"That's the story of my life—just when things start getting good, the other shoe drops."

The phrase "That's the story of my life" is used so frequently in Western culture to describe bad things we wish would stop happening that it actually sounds weird when used to describe something positive. You never hear anyone say, "That's the story of my life, I just won the lottery!" Instead, we talk about our stories in this darkly comedic, nonchalant way, as if we've been written into some big cosmic joke that we're powerless to get out of. Most of us never even consider the fact that our stories are real, that they're truly controlling our lives, and that we are actually the authors.

I had a cable repair man come to my house once who complained the entire time about how long his days were, how sore his body was, and how the power company worked him to the bone. Then he talked about his poor, dying grandma—all while I was standing there in my PJs, waiting for him to leave. Though he was clearly in pain, he seemed to enjoy telling his story. While he stood there talking, wearing a slight smile, I thought, *This is probably the perfect job for him, because it allows him to tell the same sad story every day to a new audience.*

I'm not suggesting that the cable man *likes* being miserable, but he certainly likes telling his story. Yet, even as he tells it, he isn't aware that he's inside of it, because he's blind to it.

If the cable man could *see* the existence of his story, he could reframe it. What if he talked about how lucky he is to still have his grandmother with him? What if he realized that even though he isn't happy in his job now, he has the power to either change how he relates to it or get a different job that treats him better, one that he actually enjoys?

The 3 Worst Pieces of Advice About Your Story

It seems like everybody and their dog is talking about "your story" these days. The reason so many coaches, healers, and thought leaders are talking about your story is because they listen to so many people complain about their problems every day, and are thus acutely aware of how those problems emanate from the way people tell their stories. However, that doesn't mean that everybody who's talking about your story has the best advice about how to change it. Here are the three worst pieces of advice you'll hear about your story:

1. "GET RID OF YOUR OLD STORY."

When your story is obviously holding you back, it can seem like the logical solution is to forget about it, burn it, or divorce yourself from it. While this advice is well-intentioned, getting rid of your story is simply impossible. Having a story is one of the quintessential things that makes you human. Besides, even if it *were* possible to get rid of your story, doing so would not be a wise strategy for improving your life. You'll make infinitely greater progress in achieving what you want by transforming your story in a way that leverages its power than you ever could by trying to escape it.

2. "JUST WRITE A NEW ENDING."

It's simply not possible to change your life by slapping a new ending onto your old story. That would be like trying to slap the head of a unicorn on the body of a slug and ride that abomination toward your "happily ever after." In order to change your story in a way that truly changes your life, you have to transform the *whole* of your story, so that your new Ideal Ending flows naturally out of a matching reframed beginning. If you try to just write a new ending to your old story, you'll end up with two disparate stories and the old, negative story will continue to take precedence in your mind, simply because it's stronger (as a result of having been around longer).

3. "LET GOD WRITE THE NEXT CHAPTER."

As we'll talk about in chapter 1, the ELS Method works best when you believe in a Higher Power, or when you are at least open to the possibility that one exists and wants you to thrive. That said, if you try to leave *all* the work of writing the next chapter of your life in God's hands, it will end up looking a lot like the previous chapters. After all, wasn't God writing those chapters as well? Letting God do all the work is a sneaky way to avoid taking responsibility for your own life. When instead, you take positive control over the story of your life, with loving support from the Divine, the next chapter will be *co-created* by both of you, and you'll likely find that what happens in the next chapter of your life is nothing short of miraculous.

The Relationship Between Your Thoughts and Your Story

It's widely accepted that if you want to change your life, you have to change your thoughts. However, changing your thoughts is easier said than done—they don't exist in a vacuum, and they aren't there by chance. In fact, your thoughts flow from—and are generated by—the story of your life.

Your story contains messages about what's possible for you, and the thoughts that arise in your mind are always in alignment with those messages (most of which are currently unconscious). You may be able to change your thoughts for awhile, while you're vigilantly focused on doing so, but it's not sustainable. As soon as you let your guard down and go back to daily life, your thoughts will automatically gravitate back to a set-point that is predetermined by your story.

Trying to change your thoughts without changing your story is like throwing computer software CDs at your laptop without uploading the data to your hard drive. For new data to take root in your mind, you have to transform the messages in your story into ones that generate the kinds of beneficial thoughts that will effectively change your life.

At this point, you're probably thinking, *But how can my story actually change? What's done is done. It's not like I can rewrite the past.* It's a fair question, but the scope of what you have the power to change about your story is much greater than you can imagine.

Your Personal History Is Not Set in Stone

When I speak about recreating your story, people often ask me, "Are you talking about rewriting history? Isn't that lying?" I understand the question, because "rewriting history" has a bad reputation. It's true that history has been rewritten by countless leaders and organizations in a dishonest way that distorts the truth as a means to gain power and dominion over others. But just because history has been rewritten in ill-intentioned ways doesn't mean that rewriting it is inherently bad.

In fact, when I was studying history in college, my professors *wanted* me to rewrite history, because that's the historian's job: to analyze the facts and put them together in a new way that supports a new perspective that leaves us with a *more* accurate understanding of the past, not less. This goal is especially true for historians who specialize in Native American, African American, or Women's History, because their primary aim is to address the deficiencies in our collective human story regarding people who have been grossly marginalized and misrepresented.

The reality is, there are an infinite number of "true" versions of the past. For example, historians argue to this day over who is responsible for starting the French Revolution. Some say it was started by the men who imprisoned the king. Some say it was started by the men who cut off his head. Some say it was started by the men who created The Committee of Public Safety. Others say it was started by the women who marched on Versailles, demanding food for their children. Each of these versions of history is different. Each one carries a different message. And each one is factually accurate.

Your story can also be written in an infinite number of ways, where each different version is factually accurate and carries its own message. The nature of your personal history is the same as that of history in general, because history itself is inherently fluid and alterable. While you can't escape the facts about what has happened in your past, you *can* change the *meaning* of those facts, and how they're arranged, in a way that completely changes what you believe is possible for your future.

Let me be clear. When I talk about rewriting your story, I'm not suggesting that you write a fake version that leaves out all your challenges (doing so wouldn't change your life anyway). In order to rewrite your story in a way that leads to your dreams, your story has to change in deep and authentic ways—it has to truly evolve. That requires *including* your challenges in a way that allows you to feel empowered by them. And a more empowering story is *always* a more honest one.

Your Story Can Authentically Change

Now that we've talked about why your story is changeable, let's get specific about *how* your story can change. To do that, we need to look at what your story is *made of.* Generally speaking, people think of stories as being made of things like the setting, plot, themes, and characters. But for our purposes, the two main ingredients of your story are content and perspective. You can change either ingredient (or both) while still being completely honest and authentic, and your entire story will change too.

The first ingredient of your story is content, which includes the subject matter, facts, and details that make up each moment of your life. The second ingredient of your story is perspective, which determines both how you perceive each piece of content, and how you perceive the whole of your story, as determined by how you assemble all the pieces.

Content and perspective can't be separated in your story—they become fused together just like flour and eggs when baking a cake. And even though changing one ingredient of your story will always change the other (and thus the entire story), for ease of understanding, let's look separately at how each ingredient can change.

CONTENT CAN CHANGE.

You couldn't fit every moment of your life into a written story, even if you tried. So you have to make choices about which moments to include and which ones to leave out. Each of those choices will produce a different story, a different perspective, and therefore, a different outcome.

Let's say your father abandoned you as a child. You might think that your written story would be more "positive" if you left this information out. However, the fact that he abandoned you would still be part of your internal narrative, so it would still have a powerful effect on you. Omitting this experience from your written story would leave you powerless to control how having been abandoned by your father impacts you; it would leave you powerless to consciously shape the perspective that's attached to that experience.

Since you were a child when that painful memory became locked into your unconscious narrative, and because you experienced that trauma through the eyes of a child, the default perspective attached to it would also be that of a child. A child who would be unlikely to realize that your father's decision to leave you had nothing to do with your own worthiness, and everything to do with his own issues. However, by including this "negative" experience in your written story, you empower yourself to take conscious control of the meaning assigned to it. In this case, that would mean describing the experience of being abandoned by your father through the eyes of a mature adult, who realizes that his leaving was *not* your fault, and that you are just as worthy and deserving of love as everyone else on the planet.

Alternatively, the choice you make about whether or not to include a *positive* piece of content in your written story can also vastly change your entire narrative. It's amazing how often people—myself included—initially leave out beautiful, empowering memories from their written story. This happens when the dominant story you're carrying inside is so negative that many of your truly positive experiences just don't "fit" inside of it.

Let's say you won an acting award in high school for a performance that made you feel lit-up and on-purpose. And that now, as an adult, you're pursuing a full-time career as a working actor. If you leave this positive piece of content *out* of your written story, you won't be able to automatically draw power from having won that award in your daily life.

However, if you find a home for this empowering memory in your written story, the energy of your story would change in such a way that you would book more acting roles that make you feel just like you did when you won that award. You'd naturally feel lit-up, on-purpose, and optimistic about your acting career on a daily basis—without having to try—simply because this memory had been properly integrated into your story.

Another way the content of your story can change is by emphasizing certain pieces of content more than others. For example, if you wrote at length in your story about all the bitter details of your divorce, it would have a huge impact on your perspective about what's likely to happen next in your love life. You would be more likely to attract another contentious relationship, instead of a healthy one. However, if you briefly write about your divorce in a way that harnesses the wisdom you gained from it, the outcome in your love life would be very different. You would see the potential for a wonderful new relationship, and that is why you would find it.

PERSPECTIVE CAN CHANGE.

Perspective is an even bigger wildcard in your story, because perspective itself, like history, is inherently fluid and alterable. Luckily, popular culture gives us countless examples of how one piece of content can be perceived in vastly different ways. Take the classic optical illusion where half the viewers see a beautiful young maiden and the other half see an old hag. Or the recent audio clip that went viral because half the people listening heard "Yanni," and the other half heard "Laurel." Or the photo that went viral because half of the world saw a blue and black dress, while the other half saw a gold and white one.

Similarly, you can look at any one piece of content in your history in an endless variety of ways—whether it's a wonderful memory, or an accident, failure, or heartbreak. Significant events only have the meaning that you assign to them, and that meaning can change at any time. Here's an example of how the perspective that's assigned to one line of content in your story can change, and how each different version of the story produces a completely different trajectory for your life.

Version 1: *Sean was the love of my life, and he got away.*

If you carry this version of the story about your breakup with Sean, there's a slim chance you would let yourself love anyone else as deeply as you loved him. Your mind would be predisposed to view every potential partner as someone who can't possibly be "the one," because Sean already got away. Buying into this narrative would likely lead you to be unlucky in love for the rest of your life.

Version 2: *I loved Sean so much, but since it ultimately didn't work out, I know that Source is lining up someone else who's a better match for me.*

If you carry *this* version of the story, instead, you would acknowledge your heartbreak, while honoring the fact that you learned a lot from your relationship and are that much closer to finding your ideal partner. Your mind would understand that Sean wasn't "the one" (if he had been, you would still be together), so you would view each new potential partner as someone who *could* be "the one," and that is why you would soon find your match.

In addition to being able to change your story by shifting the perspective attached to one piece of content, you can also change your story by altering how you assemble all the pieces. Think of the story of your life as a sandbox, where each grain of sand represents a piece of content, a moment in your life. You can take the same pieces of sand and put them together in a million different ways. You can build a castle, a mermaid, or a unicorn… the possibilities are endless.

While exciting, having that many choices can feel overwhelming (this is why so few people write their memoirs). However, the ELS Method will make it easy for you to choose, out of all the possibilities, what content to include in your ELS, how to assign meaning to your most significant life experiences, and how to assemble the pieces of your story in a way that truly empowers you.

You will always see your life through the lens of your current story —that will never change. However, the *lens itself* can always change, and in greater ways than you can currently imagine. If your thoughts keep gravitating back to the same negative set-point, if you're stuck in patterns that you feel powerless to change, I hope you understand by now that there is nothing wrong with you. Your mind is simply running an old story that is ready to evolve into your Essential Life Story —a short narrative that inspires you to think, feel, and behave in ways that support the magical manifestation of your Greatest Dreams.

Let's get started!

One
Preparing for the ELS Journey

The moment one definitely commits oneself,
then providence moves too.

—JOHANN WOLFGANG VON GOETHE

You picked up this book because you're ready to craft a story that leads you to the life of your dreams. By completing each step of the ELS Method, your story will be transformed in ways that free you to be, do, and have anything your heart desires. No matter who you are or what has happened in your past, you can feel lit-up by your purpose every day, make a great living doing what you love, and have the deeply fulfilling relationships that you long for. Essentially, you can *thrive*.

In order to manifest results like this though, your story must transform in a particular way—there's a formula you must follow. And to use this formula successfully, it's crucial to understand the key concepts and practices that we'll cover in this chapter.

The Tangible Things You'll Need

Ideally, you'll have each of the following before you begin:

- a nice pen
- a notebook
- a computer
- internet access
- a private, comfortable place to work
- a trusted friend or writing partner

The 4 Worldviews

Your worldview is how you believe your reality is created every day and to what extent you believe a Higher Power is involved in that creation. The ELS Method is non-sectarian and designed to work with, and strengthen, your relationship with your Higher Power, whether you believe in the Universe, God, Goddess, Jesus, Buddha, Allah, Brahman, Mother Nature, or another aspect of the Divine. For simplicity, I'll use the word Source throughout most of the book, but it's important that you refer to your Higher Power in whatever way resonates most with you.

Because the ELS Method works by helping you change your reality, your perception of how reality gets created in the first place does influence your success with the ELS Method. There are four primary worldviews, and as you read through them, notice which one resonates most with you.

1. **EVERYTHING IS RANDOM.**

   With this worldview, you believe that you have zero control over your reality. In fact, no one has control over reality according to this worldview—not even Source. This worldview isn't compatible with the ELS Method, because if you believe you have zero control over your reality, you won't believe that writing a story will change your life. If you currently subscribe to this worldview, or if part of you does, I still encourage you to move forward with the ELS Method, staying open to the possibility that your worldview may change.

2. EVERYTHING IS PREDESTINED.

According to this worldview, Source alone is responsible for creating your reality, and Source already figured out what will transpire in your life a long time ago. If you perceive your reality to be created this way, you will also believe, just like with the first worldview, that writing a story to change your life is a waste of time. But here too, I encourage you to move forward with the ELS Method anyway, staying open to the possibility that you may change your mind.

3. YOU HAVE COMPLETE CONTROL OVER YOUR REALITY.

This worldview holds that you are fully responsible for everything that happens in your life, by virtue of your own free will. If this statement describes your worldview, you can achieve great results with the ELS Method. However, there is a potential trap with this worldview: you may take more than your fair share of responsibility in your ELS for the hardships you've faced and you may judge yourself harshly for things that haven't worked out well for you. Just be aware of that trap, and if you notice yourself falling into it, try to be compassionate, understanding, and loving with yourself, instead.

4. YOU CO-CREATE YOUR REALITY WITH SOURCE.

This worldview is the most compatible with the ELS Method because it gives you a lot of power, as well as support from Source, without overburdening you with *all* of the responsibility for *everything* that happens. Under this worldview, your primary job is to be crystal clear in communicating your heart's desires to Source, while remaining open and receptive to *how* Source chooses to deliver them.

Whichever worldview you most resonate with now, you may also feel conflicted. For example, you may *want* to believe that you co-create your reality with Source, but feel torn because it doesn't always seem like Source is on your side. If that's the case, know that whenever you're struggling to manifest something, it's not because Source is conspiring against you; it's because different parts of you are in conflict about what they want, causing you to send mixed signals to Source. The ELS Method is designed to help you resolve these inner conflicts so that you can send clear signals to Source about what you want, and renew your faith that Source loves you and supports your deepest desires.

On Needs and Desires

To maximize your results with the ELS Method, it's important to understand that needs are a natural and normal part of life. Your needs include those things that are necessary for survival, such as food, water, and sleep. But for our purposes, your needs also include those things that are required for you to live a healthy and fulfilling life, such as love, respect, connection, and purposeful work. One of the foundational principles of the ELS Method is that you deserve to have all of your needs met simply because you're alive.

Desire is a more complex subject than needs, especially because you receive so many mixed messages about desire. Eastern traditions, for example, tell us that desire is the root of all suffering, while Western culture encourages us to satisfy our desires at all costs—preferably with a designer coffee in hand. Then there's the opposite message from Western culture that if you get too much of what you want, you'll be in danger of becoming "spoiled" or "entitled."

All of these contradictions can leave you wondering, *Which is it? Is desire something I'm supposed to avoid or pursue?*

The main reason desire is so confusing is that there are many different *kinds* of desire, but one word is used to describe them all. A desire to hug your child, for example, is very different from a desire to punch someone for cutting you off in traffic.

For our purposes, there are two types of desires: surface desires and heart's desires, which I will also refer to as dreams. Surface desires are old coping mechanisms for relieving pain that you weren't taught how to deal with. Anything can be the object of your surface desire, from painkillers to sex to chocolate cake—things that could actually be good for you, under different circumstances, when they aren't being used to mask a deeper pain. Satisfying your surface desires may feel good in the moment, but the good feelings won't last, because the satisfaction of your surface desire is not at true substitute for what you really want.

While satisfying your surface desires usually isn't a good idea, it's important to not be hard on yourself for having them, as that will only make them stronger. While the ELS Method isn't designed to help you satisfy surface desires, it *is* designed to help you identify and satisfy the unfulfilled needs and heart's desires, or dreams, that give rise to them.

Your heart's desires hold your purpose inside of them—they're inspired in you by Source, as a means to tell you what you're meant to be doing in life. Your dreams won't always make practical sense at first, but they will continue to call you—quietly, yet persistently—until you fulfill them. You could have a dream to do anything: ride your bike across the continent, visit every country in the world, start a family in your 50's, work with at-risk youth, direct an award-winning film, or seek enlightenment. Unlike surface desires, dreams are not a cover-up for deeper pain, though it can feel incredibly painful when you doubt, ignore, or delay them.

You may avoid your dreams for any number of reasons. You may believe that you have to accomplish other things *before* you can pursue them. Or you may carry a limiting belief that you'll have to sacrifice something (or someone) you love in order to realize your dreams. You may unconsciously feel like you have to choose between love and freedom, money and integrity, or family and success. This belief that you can only have *one* thing that's important to you stems from lack mentality, and it's a pervasive problem in our culture. The ELS Method can help you transform lack mentality into a mindset of abundance, and open you up to the possibility of having *everything* that's really important to you.

Another expression of lack mentality that can prevent you from pursuing your dreams is the belief that fulfilling them will somehow hurt—or take something away from—someone else. However, the fulfillment of any desire that truly comes from your heart would never harm anyone in any way. Love, happiness, and success are *not* limited resources. The fulfillment of your dreams is always best for you *and* everyone else.

Ultimately, only you can tell the difference between a surface desire and a dream. One person might want to become an attorney to impress people to cover up the pain of not feeling good enough (surface desire), but another might want to become an attorney because they feel deeply called to fight injustice (dream). If you have trouble deciphering a dream from a surface desire, try not to worry about it right now. You wouldn't be here if you didn't have crossed signals in your system, and moving forward with the ELS Method is what will help you reconnect to your internal wisdom, weaken your surface desires, and awaken your dreams.

The Real Cause of Suffering

Desire is often called the root of all suffering; however, desire doesn't cause suffering—how you *relate* to it does. If you relate to desire with a lot of attachment, you will suffer; but if you relate to desire with unattached optimism, it can actually be a great source of well-being and inspiration for you. Since the ELS Method is designed to help you manifest your deepest desires by creating a story that you love, it's important to understand how to ideally relate to your desires *as* you manifest them.

Say you're currently single, but dream of being with the love of your life. If you're overly attached to this desire, you might spend every day yearning for a partner, getting psychic readings about when you'll meet them, and continually focusing on their absence. In this case, you'd be relating to your desire with a lot of attachment, which would not only make you miserable, but would also carry the unwanted side effect of pushing your beloved further away, and delaying your union. Alternatively, you can accept your desire, as well as your power to manifest it, while also staying patient and appreciative of everything that's already going well in your life. This makes you a magnet for what you want.

Honoring your desires, without making your happiness dependent on their satisfaction, makes you more receptive to them. I'm not expecting you to snap your fingers and get to that place right now, but as you call forth what you want through your story, it's important to stay open and relaxed about how and when your dreams manifest. Ironically, the more patient you are, the faster and more easily your results will arrive.

Blocks and the Many Aspects of You

A block is simply the lack of momentum you experience in manifesting something that you want, because different parts of you are in conflict about that desire. In other words, one part of you wants it and another part of you doesn't. It's common to occasionally feel blocked while moving through the ELS Method, and it's important to understand what's really happening so you can move beyond it.

Let's say that one part of you dreams of recording an album, but another part of you insists that you don't have what it takes to be a recording artist. The self-doubting part of you isn't simply being cruel, it's actually trying to protect you from something that it's terrified of—something bad that might happen if you *do* record the album. It might be afraid of losing loved ones who may become jealous of your success. It might be afraid of harsh criticism. It might be afraid that you'll become arrogant.

You have many different aspects of yourself inside, such as your inner hero, mystic, saboteur, martyr, ego, and child, and you can expect most—if not all—of them to show up throughout this process. When you're experiencing inner conflict, it's common to want to isolate, dominate, or silence one aspect of yourself in an attempt to create peace. This impulse is perhaps most common when it comes to your ego, which is often referred to as a "bad" part that needs to be slayed. But all parts of you are valid—no matter how loud, mistaken, or unloving they may seem in the moment. Reacting to any part of yourself with hostility will only fuel your inner conflict, and thereby strengthen the block.

If you look deep enough, you'll find that every part of you is always coming from a place of positive intent, and that each is doing the best it can with the information it has at the time. In order to resolve a block, you have to help each part of you get what it needs, instead of making one right and the other wrong. You have to turn your attention inward and ask the different aspects of yourself, with love and curiosity, *Is there anything that you want to tell me or share with me? How are you feeling? What do you need from me?*

When you explore the needs and feelings of the different aspects of yourself with kindness, respect, and curiosity—rather than blame, shame, and judgment—you can resolve inner conflict more easily than you might expect. As you move through the process, it will become easier to relate to the different aspects of yourself in this loving way, and create inner peace amongst them. Such peaceful internal conflict resolution will allow you to harness all the precious energy that you used to spend fighting yourself to realize your dreams, instead. That's when you will become unstoppable.

The Greatest Obstacle Is Resistance

The single greatest obstacle to your success with the ELS Method is resistance to the process itself, and it manifests most often by not following the instructions, or as I call it, "skipping off the path."

In his book *The Big Leap*, author Gay Hendricks writes that humans are in the process of making an evolutionary leap to greatly expand our capacity to experience abundance, success, and love. He says that our greatest problem as a species is that we unconsciously sabotage this expansion, because we feel uncomfortable with it. As you set out on the ELS journey, it's helpful to remember this tendency we all have to limit the good things we let ourselves experience. This will help you to stay mindful of what's happening, so you can reorient toward expansion.

The Essential Life Story Process is designed to let no block escape your awareness. It will reveal to you—suspending in plain sight—whatever stands in the way of your dreams, such as hidden fears, limiting beliefs, and negative parental imprints. At the same time, the ELS Method will empower you to overcome those blocks. Because the method works so well, your greatest obstacle will not be the blocks themselves, but rather, your resistance to the greater levels of fulfillment and happiness that come naturally when you follow the instructions.

In most cases, skipping steps and ignoring instructions won't be something you'll do consciously. Every person I've coached through this process (myself included) has skipped off the path, no matter how committed they were to changing the story of their life and no matter how good they were at following instructions. It's almost comical how many times I've heard someone say, "Really? I didn't answer that question?" Or "I can't believe I missed that section!"

This process leads you to doors that are like portals of change, and when you walk through them, your life will be very different on the other side. That's why the parts of you that are resistant to change will do a Jedi mind trick on other parts of you. It's as if, with a wave of their hand and a hypnotizing stare that makes entire sentences, paragraphs, and chapters disappear from sight, they say, "There is no door here."

Even when you realize that you've wandered off the path, you may develop all sorts of justifications for "why" it's best to skip certain questions or instructions. But all of the instructions exist for a reason and I've spent thousands of hours developing, testing and optimizing the ELS Method to ensure that every time you come back to the path, after having momentarily "skipped off," you will experience breakthroughs and results.

And that's the beauty of resistance... it's a powerful indicator that you're right on the verge of a major breakthrough. So whenever you notice that you've skipped off the path, be gentle with yourself, get back on track, and get excited, because something amazing is about to happen!

Best Practices for Each Chapter

1. WRITE BY HAND, THEN ON COMPUTER.

Every chapter has its own ELS Written Exercise and it's important to complete these exercises by hand, for several reasons. First, it's more relaxing to write by hand than to type on a computer, and doing so gives you more access to the parts of your brain that process emotion. Also, writing by hand is generally slower, giving you more time for self-reflection. Once you finish writing each exercise by hand, you'll type your responses into a document, titled *ELS Written Exercises*. The reason it's so important to alternate between writing by hand and typing on the computer is that you will always see things one way that you don't the other, which means more opportunities to experience breakthroughs and evolve your perspective. Typing your ELS Written Exercises also makes it easier to receive and incorporate written feedback, and it's also necessary for using the Copy and Paste ELS Template to assemble your ELS in chapter 9.

2. READ EACH CHAPTER TWICE.

It's a good idea to get in the habit of reading each chapter before *and* after completing each of your ELS Written Exercises. Upon reading a chapter for the first time, you'll gain only an *intellectual* understanding of the information; after completing your ELS Written Exercise, you'll have an *experiential* understanding of the material, as well. When you read the chapter a second time, you'll see things you missed the first time and gain an even deeper understanding of the content that will expand your success.

3. VISIT THE ELS RESOURCE BANK.

The ELS Resource Bank is a free online library, which you can join at www.TheELSResourceBank.com, where I'll provide you with supplemental resources to enhance your ELS Journey. In it, you'll find downloadable versions of the ELS Written Exercises (with instructions to make handwriting each exercise easier), as well as a *Master ELS Written Exercises* document to make it simple to type your ELS Written Exercises into one place. You'll also see call-out boxes throughout the book that describe additional downloads that are available "in the bank."

4. RECEIVE FEEDBACK[1].

The primary purpose of getting feedback on your ELS Written Exercises, from a trusted friend or writing partner, is to make sure that you *stay on the path* and follow the instructions. It's *not* (let me reiterate: NOT!) to give you advice. So much gets revealed about your psychology while using the ELS Method that it becomes very easy—and tempting—for anyone who looks at your ELS Written

---

[1]. You *can* use the ELS Method on your own. If you decide to go that route, double or triple check your ELS Written Exercises to make sure you followed the instructions. You'll always find some way in which you skipped off the path, and getting back on the path is key!

Exercises to try to psychoanalyze or "fix you." This unsolicited advice would be a distraction from the process, so it's crucial for anyone who provides you with feedback to understand what their primary role is (to ensure that you follow the instructions). It's also crucial for you to choose a trusted friend or writing partner who won't try to "bring you back to reality" after learning about your dreams, or project their own limitations onto you. It doesn't matter if you want to become a ballerina in your eighties or build a rocket ship in your backyard—if someone tries to limit you, share this paragraph with them, and if they still aren't able or willing to be supportive, please find someone else to provide you with feedback.

 Visit www.TheELSResourceBank.com to find *Guidelines for Providing Feedback on ELS Written Exercises,* a download that you can give to anyone who provides you with feedback.

Your Commitment Statement

Each of the ELS Written Exercises in this book is transformative on its own, but it's how they all fit together in the end that provides you with the greatest opportunity to evolve. That's why it's so important to follow the *entire* process through to completion. And to do that, you need to make a commitment to the ELS Method.

Your first ELS Written Exercise is to write Your Commitment Statement, which includes how often you'll work on your ELS, where you'll write, and from whom you'll receive feedback. The recommended pace for how often you'll work is once a week or every other week, setting aside two to three hours for each session, and it's a good idea to choose the same day and time of the week, so it becomes a ritual. Many chapters can be completed in less time, but you'll hang out in some for longer. It's a good idea to work somewhere private and comfortable, so it feels less like "work" and more like self-care. My favorite place to write is curled up in bed, but yours may be laying in a hammock or sitting on your favorite chair in the living room. When it comes to who you'll receive feedback from, make sure to choose someone whom you trust implicitly. And as always, enjoy the process!

Chapter 1 ELS Written Exercise

Before you begin, create a sacred, comfortable space to work. Turn off your devices and make sure you won't be interrupted for at least an hour. Using a pen and paper, write your responses to the following questions by hand.

1. From whom will you receive feedback?

2. How often will you work on your story, and on what day of the week will you work?

3. Where (physically) will you write?

4. Write Your Commitment Statement by filling in the template below with your responses from above.

5. I'm 100% committed to completing my ELS, by working on it _____ (insert your answer for #2) at _____ (insert your answer for #3) and receiving regular feedback from _____ (insert your answer for #1).

6. Create a document titled *ELS Written Exercises* and inside of it, type the heading "My Commitment Statement." Then type your Commitment Statement underneath the header. Alternatively, you can download the *Master ELS Written Exercises* document and simply type your Commitment Statement into the space provided.

Example:

I'm 100% committed to completing my ELS, by working on it every Monday at six P.M. and receiving regular feedback from my writing partner, Jen.

7. Have a trusted friend or writing partner provide you with feedback to ensure that you followed the instructions for this ELS Written Exercise.

in the bank

Visit www.TheELSResourceBank.com to download a printable version of the *Chapter 1 ELS Written Exercise*, which includes the instructions from this chapter that you'll need to complete your exercise. You can also download the *Master ELS Written Exercises* document for typing up your responses.

Two

Crafting Your
ELS Intention

*You and everyone else, as well as all life,
emanated from the universal all-creating field of intention.*

—DR. WAYNE W. DYER

In this chapter, you'll write your ELS Intention, which is a clear and concise statement about what you want to achieve with the ELS Method. When creating your reality in partnership with Source, crafting clear intentions is your primary task. Intentions act as directives for your mind, keeping you focused on what's most important to you, and they also act as directives for Source, so it can deliver. Before I talk specifically about how to create an ELS Intention, I'd like to share a story to help you further understand the importance of having one.

In 2003, I was sitting in a motivational seminar, and the teacher showed us a video about the power of focus. Before turning it on, she told us that we would see several people standing in a circle, passing basketballs back and forth, and that our job was to count how many times we saw each basketball change hands. As I watched the video, I remember thinking, *Wow, that's a lot of basketballs flying around, I hope I don't miss any of them…*

When the movie was over, the teacher asked, "So, how many times did you see a basketball change hands?" People shouted out a bunch of different numbers: "fifty-six!" "thirty-two!" "forty-eight!" Then the teacher asked, "Now, how many of you saw the giant gorilla?"

There were about forty of us in the class that day, and all of us were confused. One guy said, "I think I might have seen a gorilla," but he wasn't sure, and the rest of us had no memory of a gorilla whatsoever. So, the teacher put the same movie on again, but this time we were all looking for a gorilla instead of basketballs. And sure enough, there he was. A man wearing a giant gorilla costume walked right into the middle of the circle of people, looked straight at the camera, shrugged his shoulders, and then walked away.[1] The power of intention is that it can direct your mind to focus so strongly on one thing (like basketballs) that you're unable to see other things that are right in front of your face (like a gorilla).

As we talked about in the introduction, you could write a million different versions of your life story. In order to write the version of your story that supports your dreams coming true, you need a concise, regular reminder of what your dreams *are*. Your ELS Intention will provide you with that reminder and it will also direct your mind to look for and find everything in your story that stands in the way of your dreams, so that those obstacles can be overcome.

Instructions for Crafting Your ELS Intention

You'll craft your ELS Intention by filling in the blanks of the following template: *Writing my ELS is a _____ process that results in _____, _____, _____, and _____*. You'll simply fill in the first blank with the kind of process you want to have, and the next blanks with

---

1. *Selective Attention Test*. Dir. Daniel J. Simons. *The Invisible Gorilla*. Simons and Chabris, 2010. Web. 2016

the internal and external results you would like. A completed example looks like this: *Writing my ELS is an enlightening process that results in my feeling totally confident in myself, recording an album, going on tour, and being happily married to the love of my life.* Here's a more detailed list of instructions for crafting an optimal ELS Intention:

1. **DESCRIBE HOW YOU WANT TO EXPERIENCE THE PROCESS.**

   The best way to describe how you want to experience the ELS Method is to start with describing how you *don't* want to experience the process, or in other words, how you're afraid the process might go. Let's say you've bought a lot of self-help books in the past that you never finished, so you're afraid you won't finish this book either, and therefore won't finish your ELS, itself. You can counteract that fear by stating, *Writing my ELS is a deeply engaging process,* because when that is true, you *will* complete it. Ask yourself, *What am I afraid of feeling or experiencing in this process?* And then write into your ELS Intention what you want *instead* of that fear. Choose words that directly contradict any fears you have about how the process might go. If you're afraid the process will be a drag, claim that it will be energizing. If you're afraid that the changes brought about by the ELS Method will be too abrupt, claim that the process will be gentle. If you're afraid that it won't work for you, claim that it will. Try to use no more than two words when describing the way in which you want to experience the process, because the more concise your ELS Intention is, the more powerful it will be.

2. **NAME THE INTERNAL RESULTS YOU WANT TO EXPERIENCE.**

   Internal results are changes that you experience inside of yourself, such as changes in how you feel and what you believe. For example, one of my clients had a strong pattern of not listening to her intuition, relying instead on the advice of others. She didn't want the ELS Method to reinforce her pattern of prioritizing external advice over internal knowing. I told her that while yes, the ELS Method was designed by someone else—and following it *could* be seen as taking outside advice—it was designed to give her greater access to her own inner wisdom. So, she added the following internal result to her ELS Intention: *prioritizing my intuition over outside advice.* It's important to choose internal results that describe the opposite of any long-standing negative, internal patterns you may be struggling with. If you have a deep-seated pattern of putting others' needs before your own, your main internal result might be: *having the courage to put myself first.* If you're always down-playing your personal successes, the main internal result you describe might be: *appreciating and valuing my own accomplishments.*

3. **NAME THE EXTERNAL RESULTS YOU WANT TO EXPERIENCE.**

External results are the more tangible things you want, and they usually fall into the categories of love, success, money, and creativity. Examples include: *being in the best shape of my life, starting a family, becoming a bestselling author, earning six figures as an actress, recording my first album,* and *founding a non-profit for protecting the rainforest.* An external result can be anything your heart desires, as long as it's tangible and specific. For example, financial goals are best described using numbers so that it's easier to know when you've achieved them, as in *earning 100k a year,* instead of *making good money.* If you have a fitness goal, write down your ideal weight, body fat index, or how many miles you want to be able to run, instead of just *having great health.*

4. **REVISIT YOUR INTERNAL RESULTS AFTER NAMING YOUR EXTERNAL ONES.**

After you clarify the external results you want, revisit your internal results to see if they need to be updated to better support your external results. For example, if one of your external results is to be a published author, ask yourself if anything needs to shift internally for you to achieve that external goal and if so, include it in your ELS Intention. You may have originally written *confidence* as the internal result you wanted, but realize that when you become an author, you'll need to do book readings, and you're terrified of public speaking. If that's the case, you could update your internal result to be: *feeling relaxed and confident while speaking to an audience.*

5. **ESSENTIALIZE YOUR RESULTS.**

It's common for the first draft of your ELS Intention to include a long list of internal or external results, but an overly long ELS Intention is actually a sneaky way to dilute your power and skip off the path. If your first draft is long, spend some time marrying similar words and phrases, choosing those that can best stand in for others. Here's an example of a lengthy first draft: *I want to stop doubting myself and being my own worst enemy. I want to stop torturing myself and telling myself how bad, ugly, and worthless I am. I want to be my own best friend. I want to encourage myself and feel confident that I can achieve my dreams and feel confident that I'm worthy and deserving of them.* An essentialized version of the above might be: *Writing my ELS is a successful process that results in my feeling confident that I can achieve my dreams and becoming my own best friend.* Notice that in the essentialized version, none of the initial results were left out, they were merely referred to in fewer words. When your intention is this concise, you may even find yourself reciting it in your mind when you're driving down the road or washing dishes—which makes it even more powerful. Also, remember that you can include results in many areas of your life, such as your career, health, and relationships, just take the time to ensure each result is described concisely.

6. USE POSITIVE LANGUAGE.

Your unconscious mind and Source don't hear negative qualifiers, like "never," "no," "un," "non," or "stop;" they hear the words that negative qualifiers are *attached to*. The Titanic, for example, was heralded across the globe as being "unsinkable." However, the focus of that word is actually *sinkable*... and we all know how that story ended. That said, negative language—describing what you *don't* want—is a great place to begin when clarifying what you *do* want. If you have difficulty coming up with positively-worded internal and external results that you're excited about, start by describing what you're tired of experiencing in your life and then turn it around. For example, you can turn *being sick* into *feeling healthy and vibrant*. You can turn *being in debt* into *being financially solvent*. And you can turn *never having another dead-end relationship* into *being happily married to the love of my life*.

7. BE VERY SPECIFIC!

If you put *vague* out to Source, you'll get *vague* in response. So, instead of writing vague results, like *creative success, financial freedom*, and *dream career*, specifically describe what each of those things look like for you. To make *creative success* more specific, ask yourself, *If I did have creative success, how would I know it? What would I be doing?* The meaning of creative success can be vastly different for different people. For one person, it could mean *carving a totem pole* and for another, *touring the country as a stand-up comedian*. It's much easier for Source to help you manifest results when you are ultra specific in your ELS Intention.

8. WRITE SIMPLY.

It can be tempting to write your ELS Intention in a poetic and flowery way, as in, *Writing my ELS frees me to delve into the deepest depths of my hindered soul, freeing myself to shatter all misconceptions and rise victorious above all barriers…* you get the picture. It's hard to point out anything "wrong" with such poetic and flowery statements, however, they're actually a sneaky way of being vague, and therefore skipping off the path. Remember, the point of your ELS, and therefore your ELS Intention, is personal transformation, not to impress anyone; so describe the results you want to experience as simply and directly as you can.

9. FOCUS ON THE RESULTS (NOT ON HOW THEY WILL MANIFEST).

Another trap you can fall into when creating your ELS Intention is getting hung up on *how* your results will manifest. You don't have to have any earthly idea how they will manifest; you just have to know what you want. When you get attached to the "how," you close yourself off from allowing your dreams to arrive in unexpected ways, and Source is notorious for bringing you what you want in more creative ways than you can imagine! That's because it knows—so much better than one person ever could—all of the available options for manifestation. You'll know that you've fallen into the trap of getting hung up on the "how" if you notice any "so that" clauses in your ELS Intention. "So that" clauses put unnecessary conditions on manifesting your results by trying to control the order in which they come to you. For example: *Writing my ELS is an enlightening process that results in my feeling good about myself, **so that** I can finally make good decisions in love, **so that** I can finally have the relationship I've always wanted.* That ELS Intention would best be re-written as: *Writing my ELS is an enlightening process that results in my feeling good about myself,* *making good decisions in love, and having the relationship I've always wanted.*

10. COUNTER YOUR FEARS.

It's common to feel resistant to naming what you want in your ELS Intention, because you're afraid of what might happen that's *negative* if you get what you want. If you notice that you're tiptoeing around naming an ideal result, ask yourself, *What might happen that's negative if I get this particular result that I want?* While that might sound like a ridiculous question at first, if you sit with it, the answer will come. Then, write down what you're afraid of, and write *the opposite of that* into your ELS Intention. Let's say you're afraid that your marriage will suffer if your career takes off. You can counter that fear in your ELS Intention by declaring, *My marriage gets even stronger as my career takes off.*

11. ALLOW FOR ABUNDANCE.

The reason you even *have* fears like the ones we just discussed in #10 above, is that you're a product of our culture. As we talked about in chapter 1, lack mentality is a pervasive problem in our culture. Most of us have been taught since birth that we can have only *one* of what we want—whether it's *one* piece of candy, *one* favorite color, or *one* creative passion. The cult of "just one!" makes it incredibly common to feel afraid that you'll pay the price if you ask for too much and have to choose one thing that's important to you over another. Let's say that when you write down wanting to be married to the love of your life, you feel a strong fear that you'll have to give up your career as a singer to have that kind of relationship. The solution is to create an ELS Intention that includes *both* things you want. Doing so helps you reverse the belief that you have to choose, and allows you to build a story where you can have it *all*. For example, you could write, *Writing my ELS is an engaging process that results in my being with the love of my life and having the singing career of my dreams.* Including *two* results that used to feel mutually exclusive will open you to the possibility of having true abundance.

12. **MAKE SURE YOUR ELS INTENTION STRETCHES YOU.**

Make sure that the results you list in your ELS Intention are those that you *most want to manifest right now*—things that you aren't already experiencing, or that you aren't experiencing to the degree you would like. If one of your desired results is *being on TV*, ask yourself, *Have I already been on TV?* If the answer is yes, then this result isn't stretching you to create something new. Perhaps what you really want is a more prominent role, such as a series regular on a major network. It's very common to name things in your ELS Intention that are *close* to what you want, but tiptoe around your true ideal. You know you're doing this when you read your ELS Intention and it doesn't move you emotionally. If it falls flat, just ask yourself, *What drew me to this process in the first place? What was I most wanting to change?* Even further, ask yourself, *If a genie fell down out of the sky right now and could grant my any wish, what would I wish for?* You have to be honest with yourself in order to craft an ELS Intention that pushes the boundaries of what's possible for you. You'll know you've achieved that when reading your ELS Intention makes you ask yourself—with both excitement and a little fear—*Is this even possible?* You'll know that you've stretched yourself even more when reading your ELS Intention moves you to tears.

What if I Don't Know What I Want?

If you don't know what you want right now, that's okay! You may have been drawn to the ELS Method because you know you want something *more*, but you don't know exactly what that is yet. If that's the case, the best ELS Intention for you (for now) will be something like: *Writing my ELS is an enlightening process that results in my feeling crystal clear about what I want in all areas of my life and having the courage to go for it.* As soon as you *do* become clear about what you want, re-read this chapter and update your ELS Intention using the Instructions for Crafting Your ELS Intention.

Getting your ELS Intention as dialed in as you can in this step of the process is important, because you'll get faster and better results that way. But you don't have to get it "perfect" before moving onto the next chapter. Your ELS Intention is a moving target, meant to continually evolve as you move through the process. You may not be ready to even acknowledge certain dreams—let alone manifest them—until deeper into the process. But as soon as you are ready, you'll need to integrate those dreams into your ELS Intention. Additionally, some of your results will manifest early on in the process, and when they do, you'll need to replace them with what you want to manifest *next*.

in the bank

Visit www.TheELSResourceBank.com to find *A Step-by-Step Example of How an ELS Intention Evolves*, where I provide an example of how one client's ELS Intention became progressively stronger through four different versions—complete with an explanation of what we changed and why.

The Magic Will Begin Right Away

When your ELS Intention is powerful and dialed in, it will immediately begin to shift things in your daily life. Many of my clients have manifested major results—like signing a book deal and meeting their life partner—simply from including those results in their ELS Intention, before moving any further through the ELS Method. So don't be surprised if the same happens to you.

Your ELS Intention will also act as a magnet, drawing to your attention not only everything in your written story that needs to evolve, but everything in your life—which is a reflection of your written story—that needs to evolve, as well. Anything inside of you that is *not* a match for your ELS Intention—like an old pattern or belief that no longer serves you—will intensify and bubble up to the surface of your life, like oil on water, so that you can easily see and transform it.

After creating your ELS Intention, don't be surprised if an old flame suddenly calls you out of the blue, or if you run into your former best friend at the grocery store. That's Source's way of saying, "The results you wrote into your ELS Intention are wonderful and I want you to have them! See how these things from your past aren't a match for what you want now?" Sometimes, Source will briefly reunite you with such people as a reminder that you have unfinished business with them, so that you can resolve it with the ELS Method (there's an entire chapter on resolving unfinished business coming up soon).

Such magical "coincidences" may feel weird at first, but they're actually a natural and normal outcome of using the ELS Method. And the more you acknowledge the connection between your ELS Intention and the magic that's unfolding in your life, the more Source will bend over backwards to help make your ELS Intention come true.

Path Skipping in Chapter 2

As we covered in chapter 1, resistance is a natural part of the ELS Method, and it usually manifests as "skipping off the path." The most common way to skip off the path in this stage of the process is by not following the Instructions for Crafting your ELS Intention. Another way is to resist writing your ELS Intention altogether, because you feel like intentions in general are too rigid and controlling. I've heard people say things like, "What if there's something out there that's even better for me? Shouldn't I let Source determine what happens in my life?" But creating intentions isn't rigid or controlling; it's creative. Your innate creative power is a gift from Source that's meant to empower you to co-create your reality *with* Source. You're partners. As long as you're open to how your ELS Intention manifests, and willing to update it as Source reveals more of what's possible, you are being anything but rigid.

Chapter 2 ELS Written Exercise

Before you begin, create a sacred, comfortable space to work. Turn off your devices and make sure you won't be interrupted for at least an hour. Read your ELS Intention aloud, and update it, if needed. Using a pen and paper, write your responses to the following questions by hand.

1. What fears or concerns do you have about how the process of using the ELS Method will go for you?

2. How would you ideally like to experience the process instead?

3. What specific internal results would you like?

4. What specific external results would you like?

5. Are there any other internal results that you need to experience in order for your external results to come true? If so, adjust your answer to #3 above.

6. Using the template below, create your ELS Intention.

   Writing my ELS is a _____ (insert your answer from #2) process that results in my feeling _____ (insert your answers from #3); and _____, _____, and _____ (insert your answers from #4).

Example:

Writing my ELS is a deeply engaging and inspiring process that results in my feeling happy and peaceful every day; being happily married to the love of my life; having a deeply loving home; and making seven figures a year producing films that change the world.

7. Have a trusted friend or writing partner provide you with feedback to ensure that you followed the instructions for this ELS Written Exercise.

8. Open your *ELS Written Exercises* document and below your Commitment Statement, type the header "My ELS Intention, Today's Date" and type your ELS Intention underneath. Alternatively, if you're using the *Master ELS Written Exercises* document, just type your ELS Intention into the space provided.

in the bank

Visit www.TheELSResourceBank.com to download a printable version of the *Chapter 2 ELS Written Exercise*, which includes the instructions from this chapter that you'll need to complete your exercise.

Three
Revealing Your Old Story

Know from whence you came.
If you know from whence you came,
there are absolutely no limitations to where you can go.

—JAMES BALDWIN

In order to actually change the old story that's holding you back, you first have to be able to *see it*. In this chapter, you'll complete an exercise called your 5-Page Freewrite, which will provide you with much of the raw content that you'll use in later chapters to craft your ELS. Your 5-Page Freewrite will also reveal your old story and bring hidden patterns in your psychology to light.

One reason your 5-Page Freewrite will reveal your hidden psychology is because it's a *short, yet comprehensive* story that allows you to easily see unconscious patterns that you simply can't see in any other way. The even deeper reason though, that your 5-Page Freewrite will pull back the curtain on your unconscious mind, is because your ELS Intention will dictate what comes out of your pen—it's designed to direct your mind to look for and find everything in your history that is standing in the way of your dreams.

My client Tara had already written her story several times with other methods before using the ELS Method, and when she wrote her 5-Page Freewrite, she was shocked by how different this version was from all the previous ones. Tara saw strong, negative patterns and beliefs in her story that she was previously unaware of—patterns and beliefs that were clearly preventing her from achieving her dreams. For example, Tara discovered the unconscious belief that she had to choose between having a family and having a career (even though she really wanted both); this awareness explained why she was always going back and forth between being obsessed over a man and being a workaholic. Tara also realized how much she wanted to be a writer—a dream that had been easy to deny before seeing in her 5-Page Freewrite, the sheer number of times she had begun taking writing classes before dropping out shortly thereafter.

Because Tara wrote her story using the ELS Method, she saw what she intended to see—everything that needed to change in her story so that she could realize her dreams, which for her, meant having both a loving family *and* a fulfilling career as a writer. Like Tara, you can expect to see everything that needs to change in your story, so that you can realize your own dreams and gain even greater clarity about what they are.

On Freewriting

When I first wrote this book, I primarily focused in this chapter on trying to convince you that you already have a story inside of you, which is *why* it's so easy to freewrite. However, with time I learned that people rarely need to be convinced that they already have a story. I've never had a client report having writer's block in this stage of the process. Everyone's 5-Page Freewrites just flow right out. What people actually need more help with is coping with what they discover about themselves once that story is revealed (we'll get to that soon).

Nevertheless, let's briefly review the concept of freewriting, which you'll use to complete your 5-Page Freewrite. And the best explanation of freewriting, in my opinion, comes from author Stephen King. In his book *On Writing: A Memoir of the Craft*, King describes the process of freewriting as something that he simply allows to happen. He explains that he doesn't create his stories, he channels them through his pen, as his stories already exist beyond time and space. King never knows what's going to happen on the next page, let alone in the next sentence, and he doesn't need to. His job is to merely uncover his stories, like an archaeologist unearths bones.

The process of freewriting is the same whether you're writing fiction or your own story. In both cases, you're putting your pen down on paper and letting out a story that already exists. However, it's even easier to freewrite your story than it is to freewrite a work of fiction, because your story is right there under the surface—you don't have to do any digging to find it, you just put your pen down and it pours right out. Writing your 5-Page Freewrite in this way, without planning what you'll write ahead of time, is liberating, because it takes all of the pressure off of you.

Instructions for Writing Your 5-Page Freewrite

Your 5-Page Freewrite is the short version of your life history, from birth to present, which reveals the dominant, unconscious narrative that's currently reigning in your mind. The events you'll write about will be subconsciously linked to repeating patterns in your life that you'll need to become aware of, and transform, in order to realize your dreams.

1. **SET A TIMER FOR ONE HOUR.**

   Before writing your 5-Page Freewrite, you'll set the intention to write a 5-page story, in one continuous flow, and you'll set a timer to complete the exercise in one hour. If it feels impossible to fit all the details of your entire life story into a mere five pages, you're right—it's not possible. But that's the point. Your system will naturally prioritize what to include in those five pages, and you'll learn as much about yourself from what you *leave out* of your 5-Page Freewrite as from what you *include*. And because your aim is to cover your entire abridged history in only five pages, it'll be obvious when you've gone off on a tangent and you'll naturally get back to moving the story forward at a steady pace. The length and time-limit of your 5-Page Freewrite are important; they're safeguards built into the ELS Method to eliminate the possibility that writing your story will make you feel worse instead of better.

2. DON'T STOP TO THINK.

As we already talked about, freewriting your story is liberating because it takes all of the pressure off of you, but it's also imperative not to plan what you'll write ahead of time, or stop to think while you're writing. To get an honest snapshot of what's happening behind the scenes of your mind, you need to see the most uncensored version of the story that you're carrying inside—the one that naturally comes out on paper when you *don't* stop to think about it. If, as you're freewriting, you realize that you missed something important on the timeline, it's fine to briefly mention—out of chronological order—what you left out, but don't sit there and try to think of things you may have missed. And if you find yourself debating the truth of what you're writing as it comes out of your pen, just notice that internal questioning and keep moving forward. For example, if you're writing the sentence, *I was a really good girl when I was little,* and you notice yourself wondering if that's true, don't try to figure out the answer. You can write, *Wait, I'm not sure that's true,* but then move on and write about what happened next. Later chapters are specifically designed to help you discern what's most true for you. For now, what's most important is to see what does or doesn't automatically come out of your pen.

3. **WRITE IN CHRONOLOGICAL ORDER.**

It's common to want to skip around in chronological time as you write your 5-Page Freewrite, especially because foreshadowing and flashbacks are storytelling tools you see in books and movies all the time. But I don't advise you to skip around chronologically in this version of your story or in your ELS itself, once it's assembled in chapter 9. Moving back and forth in time is another way to skip off the path, because it can muddy up the story and make simple truths hard to see. If you notice yourself breaking from chronological order as you write your 5-Page Freewrite—such as by immediately following an embarrassing childhood memory with a comment about what you currently feel the meaning of that experience was for you—get back on track by writing about the events of your life, in chronological order, without reflecting on them from your current vantage point. There is a time and place for such reflections later in the process.

4. **WRITE FOR YOUR IDEAL READER.**

Before you begin, imagine that you'll be writing for your Ideal Reader—someone who is empathetic, nonjudgmental, and has no previous knowledge about your history. Writing for your Ideal Reader will help you write the simple truth about what's happened in your life and how you feel about it. Your ELS is for *you*, but when you imagine writing it for a completely empathetic witness, your story will come out more clearly and honestly than it would if you wrote it for your eyes only. If you can't think of someone like this, feel free to choose me as your Ideal Reader. I may not read your story in real time, but I'd be happy to stand in energetically as your witness, and I promise I won't judge.

5. **DON'T EDIT (YET).**

It's important to resist the temptation to edit your 5-Page Freewrite in this stage, either while you're writing it or before moving on to the next chapter. The point of this chapter is to get an inside view of the story that's running your life so that it can begin to evolve—it has nothing to do with creating a great piece of literature or even a cohesive story. The story that comes out of you may be confusing, choppy, or incoherent, and that's totally fine! Resist the temptation to go back and change things about your 5-Page Freewrite that you don't like, especially because removing negative experiences from your written story won't erase them from the story that's inside of you. You won't be able to transform these experiences and their effect on you (in later chapters) if you've already erased them. For now, simply reveal and reflect on your old story—as it is.

What You'll Notice

It's not always easy to see your old story in writing. I can't count how many times I've had a client lament to me about what they saw in their 5-Page Freewrite. One client said, "It's a mess! This isn't even a story. It's just random thoughts about bad things that have happened to me. And bad things I've done." Another said, "Oh my God, *this* is my backstory? This is the story I've been telling myself all these years? It's SO negative! I thought I'd worked through all of this stuff!"

You may find that your ex is starring in your story, despite the fact that you broke up ten years ago. You might realize that you act more like your parents than you thought you did. You might see patterns of dating down, playing small, or giving more than you receive. Or you might see patterns that swing to the other extreme—where you take advantage of people, behaving in ways that don't represent the kind of person you really are.

The heavy emotions and painful patterns that show up in your 5-Page Freewrite, and the duration of time that you spend writing about people who have hurt you, are a testament to the fact that time doesn't always heal. And that contrary to what you previously thought, you're *still* not "over" many of the things that you thought you were. When people have hurt you without making amends, and when bad things have happened to you without meaning having been assigned to them, it leaves a psychic wound that shows up in your story; it's your system's way of letting you know that you still need to heal. Each painful part of your story is begging to be reframed, to be given a deeper, more honest, and more empowering meaning.

Another thing you'll notice is that many of the positive experiences and relationships from your history will be missing from your 5-Page Freewrite. You might even notice that *all* of the positives are missing. I've had clients not mention their (wonderful) partners, and clients completely leave out their greatest professional achievements (which they were actually quite proud of). The missing positives in your story explain why you get stuck in negative patterns, and let you know that you need to integrate these missing positives back into your story, which you will do in later stages of the process.

All that said, you may still wonder why your 5-Page Freewrite is *so* negative. One answer is that you're a product of your culture. Turn on any mainstream news channel and you'll find plenty of evidence for how negative our collective human story can be. Sometimes you'll leave positive experiences out of your story simply because they're at odds with the dominant vibration of our collective story; it's difficult to have a positive story in a culture with a predominantly negative one. However, once you take conscious control of your own narrative, you'll raise not only the vibration of your own story, but also the vibration of our collective one.

Alternatively, *if your story is mostly positive*, and it's not because you're avoiding the negative, allow yourself to be grateful—without feeling guilty! And don't make the mistake of feeling like the positive state of your story means that there's no need to continue using the ELS Method. One of my clients dreamt of becoming a well-known journalist, but she unfortunately stopped at this stage of the process. Her 5-Page Freewrite reminded her so strongly of how blessed she was to have had a happy childhood and supportive parents, and to now have a loving husband with whom she travels the world—that she felt guilty asking for more. If she'd continued on, though, she could have used the ELS Method to expand on all that happiness and have a fulfilling career as a journalist who makes a great difference in the world, as well. So if your story is mainly positive, know that you're always worthy of greater expansion, and that Source *wants* you to keep expanding.

How to Deal with What's Revealed

Your 5-Page Freewrite is like a blueprint of your own psychology, and the good news about the not-so-great things that it will reveal to you is that from the moment you become aware of them, they'll begin to change. Awareness itself sets change in motion.

My client Colleen had a breakthrough while writing her 5-Page Free-write: she had a habit of intensely judging others for behaviors that she was actually guilty of herself. This realization was upsetting, and it made her question *everything*. She felt like her old story had been torn into a million pieces and thrown up into the air, which left her wondering, *What IS my story anyway? If I was wrong to judge others (because I was doing the same thing), what else am I wrong about?* However, Colleen was also excited, because she knew that she was already way less likely to continue judging others for what she was doing herself, since she could now see the pattern clearly.

The negative patterns you become aware of, by virtue of writing your Five-Page Freewrite, will start to change immediately, simply through your expanded awareness and inclination to make different choices moving forward. That said, it's okay to feel regret for time that seems wasted and things you wish you had done differently, and you may even need to have a good cry or laugh about what you see—it can be tragic and comical all at the same time when you suddenly see a truth that could have saved you *years* of agony if you'd only seen it sooner.

However, it's very important not to blame, shame, or punish yourself for any negative patterns, habits, or beliefs you see in your story, for if you do, you will reinforce the very thing you're wanting to change. Instead, have compassion for yourself and forgive yourself for not having already changed what you couldn't even *see* yet. Be loving and understanding with yourself no matter what you see in your 5-Page Freewrite, and what feels unpleasant to you will immediately begin to change.

Also, don't be surprised if you suddenly feel a strong urge to clean out your closets at this stage of using the ELS Method. After you see old things inside of your story that you don't need any more, you will start seeing old things in your environment that you don't need anymore either, because your life and your story are mirrors of one another.

Patterns That Manifest in Writing and How They Can Change

Some of the limiting patterns that become evident in your 5-Page Free-write will be illuminated by the *way* you write your story. The strongest example I've seen of a pattern in someone's life being mirrored in their writing was in my client Sean's 5-Page Freewrite. Sean had a pattern of feeling like an outsider in his own life, and this pattern could be seen in the way he wrote his story. He wrote, for example: *Sean always wanted to be part of a group but never seemed to get further than being an outsider or orbiter, he was only let in to the core group when he was useful or good for a laugh.*

Sean's 5-Page Freewrite came out in third person, as if he was literally outside of his own story. Because this pattern was unconscious, he didn't even notice that he was writing in third person until I pointed it out. In later stages of the process, Sean converted his entire story to first person, so the previous excerpt became: *I always wanted to be part of a group but never seemed to get further than being an outsider or orbiter, and I was only let in to the core group when I was doing things for them or was good for a laugh.*

The shift Sean experienced by changing the words from third to first person had a profound effect on his life. Shortly after, he started speaking from a more empowered place, saying things like, "This is my life. I get to choose what happens." He started cutting ties with people who treated him poorly, caring less about what they thought and more about what made him feel good. He said, "I can see clearly now that it used to feel like I was watching my own life through a window with my nose pressed up against the glass, and now I'm on the inside."

While you won't work on transforming patterns that manifest through writing until later stages of the process, I bring it up now because I want you to understand that it's normal to see such patterns *and* I want you to understand that they can, and will, change.

Revisiting (and Adding to) The Best Practices

In chapter 1, we covered the best practices for each chapter: write by hand then computer; read each chapter twice; visit the ELS Resource Bank; and receive feedback. In this chapter, we're adding two additional best practices: review your ELS Intention in case it needs an update, and record your breakthroughs and results.

Before we talk about the two additional best practices, I'd like to briefly review the first one—writing by hand first then on the computer—because it's particularly important when writing your 5-Page Freewrite. My client Benji said to me one day, "I wrote the handwritten draft of my 5-Page Freewrite two weeks ago, but when I typed it up last night, it felt very different. In the handwritten draft, parts of my story were wrapped up in these weird shame burritos that hurt to look at. But when I typed it up, it was easier to look at and I actually had a breakthrough: I want to start a blog because writing feels central to my calling." This breakthrough happened because the story was written first by hand

and then on computer. Benji needed to process the pain that came up while writing his 5-Page Freewrite by hand before he could have the breakthrough he experienced while typing it.

After Benji realized that he wanted to become a blogger, he needed to add that tangible result to his ELS Intention (along with the internal result of trusting that what he has to share is important), which brings us to the first additional best practice: updating your ELS Intention. As I mentioned in chapter 2, your ELS Intention is a moving target, meant to continually evolve as you move through the process. That's why it's so important to make updating it a best practice for each chapter, revisiting the Instructions for Crafting Your ELS Intention, as needed. Every time you experience a breakthrough—when you remember a dream you'd forgotten about or see an old pattern you were previously unaware of—you may need to update your ELS Intention, adding a new result or replacing an existing result with a more compelling one.

The next best practice is recording the breakthroughs and results you experience under a header called "Breakthroughs and Results" at the bottom of your *ELS Written Exercises* document. Breakthroughs are realizations that you have about the story of your life at any time while using the ELS Method. They can happen while writing or reflecting on your story, but they can also happen while doing things that feel completely unrelated to the ELS Method, like driving, taking a shower, or having a conversation with a friend. Results are tangible improvements that were written into your ELS Intention before they manifested in your life, or improvements that feel related to the breakthroughs you've experienced. Breakthroughs and results are powerful on their own, but integrating them into your story—as you'll do in later stages—will greatly magnify their impact. It's important to record breakthroughs and results right when they happen so you don't forget them, because they'll play an important role in later stages of the process.

in the bank   Visit www.TheELSResourceBank.com to find *Best Practices for Each Chapter*, where all six best practices can be easily downloaded for reference.

Path Skipping in Chapter 3

It's common after writing your 5-Page Freewrite, even with everything I've shared about how changeable your story is, to find yourself thinking, *Well, this is just the way it is. This is the story of my life. These are the facts. I can't change them.* If you allow this doubt, or resistance, to keep you from moving forward in the process, it becomes a form of Path Skipping. Remember, completing your 5-Page Freewrite is like revealing a blueprint of your own psychology; it's meant to gauge where your mind is, spot hidden patterns, and generate new awareness. The changeable nature of your story will become clearer with each step of the process, and you don't have to change any part of your story before you're ready.

Another reason you may doubt the ELS Method is that it's a way of avoiding the process, so that you can continue confirming your old story (because you have a lot of attachment to it!). The good news is that once you transform your old story into a new one that inspires you, you will automatically confirm the new story in the same way that you used to confirm the old one, only your new story will support your Greatest Dreams.

Chapter 3 ELS Written Exercise

Before you begin, create a sacred, comfortable space to work. Turn off your devices and make sure you won't be interrupted for at least an hour. Read your ELS Intention aloud, and update it, if needed. Then, complete the following:

1. Write your 5-Page Freewrite by hand, using the Instructions for Writing Your 5-Page Freewrite.

2. After you've completed your 5-Page Freewrite, take a break, and then read over your story. What new awareness have you gained? What limiting beliefs or patterns do you notice? Write your realizations down underneath your 5-Page Freewrite.

3. Open your *ELS Written Exercises* document and under your ELS Intention, write the header "5-Page Freewrite, Today's Date" and type your 5-Page Freewrite underneath.

4. Below that, type the heading "Breakthroughs and Results," and follow it with a bulleted list of the realizations that you wrote by hand in answer to question #2 above. Also, record any results you've experienced since beginning the ELS Method. Make sure each breakthrough and result you list starts with the date it occurred, as having your breakthroughs and results in chronological order will be important later.

5. Review your ELS Intention and consider updating the internal or external results you'd like to experience with any new desired results that you got in touch with while writing or reflecting on your 5-Page Freewrite.

6. Ask a trusted friend or writing partner for feedback on your 5-Page Freewrite, remembering that it will be easier for them than it is for you, to spot overarching patterns that you haven't been able to see because of how close you are to your story.

in the bank

Visit www.TheELSResourceBank.com to download a printable version of the *Chapter 3 ELS Written Exercise,* which includes the instructions from this chapter that you'll need to complete your exercise.

Four

Upgrading Your
Parental Modeling

*Children learn more from what you are
than what you teach.*

—W.E.B. DUBOIS

Most animals learn how to survive by emulating their parents: it's how birds learn to fly, bears learn to catch fish, and horses learn to run from danger. Nature's brilliant design allows babies to directly benefit from hundreds of thousands of years of evolution. Humans are also predisposed to act like their parents. However, due to many factors, which include rapid technological advancements, the patterns that worked for your parents, grandparents, and ancestors are likely very different from those that will best serve you now.

Even if you think of yourself as being very different from your parents, the patterns of thought, feeling, and behavior that you engage in every day likely echo those of your parents more than you think. While that likelihood may feel uncomfortable to consider (especially if your relationship with your parents is challenging), denying or ignoring their influence won't make it go away—it will actually make it stronger, by leaving it outside of your conscious control.

When my daughters were very young, they often said things like, "Mommy, I want the red one, because that's your favorite color" and "I want to dye my hair black so it looks like yours." The same kind of thing happens in every household. Children instinctively want to copy their parents, not only because they're wired to do so, but because it's one of their most powerful ways of saying, "I love you."

When you are blocked or stalled in the achievement of your dreams, it's usually because parts of you (often quite young parts) are attached to being like your parents in ways that are incompatible with the achievement of your dreams. In order to make room in your story for what you truly want next, you have to let the young parts of yourself know that it's okay to be different from your parents in any way that serves you, and that it's also okay to be the *same* as your parents in any way that serves you. You have to provide yourself with healthier ways of connecting to your parents, and to do that, you first have to bring what your parents modeled for you into the light of your conscious awareness and sort out what works for you from what doesn't.

If you want financial abundance in your life, you may struggle to achieve it because your parents never did. If you want a healthy, loving relationship, you may flounder because your parents were at each other's throats every day. If you want to share your creative projects with the world in highly visible ways, you may feel blocked because your parents never followed their own creative dreams. The good news is that no matter what your parents modeled, you have the power to upgrade your own internal parental modeling, take control of the influence your parents have over the story of your life, and free yourself to truly be your own person—all while allowing even *more* love to flow between you and your parents.

The 3 Categories of Parental Relationships

You likely fall into one of three categories when it comes to your relationship with your parents: the Absent Category, the Challenging

Category, or the Great Category. While it may seem like the Great Category is better than the previous two categories, each comes with unique challenges, and the ELS Method can empower you to craft a story that leads to your Greatest Dreams no matter which category you find yourself in. Whichever category you most identify with, please read each, as there is a lot of crossover amongst them.

THE ABSENT CATEGORY

If one or both of your biological parents are absent from your life, your relationship with them falls into the Absent Category. This can happen if you were placed for adoption, if your parent abandoned you, if you're estranged, or if they have passed away. It's important to remember that even if your parents are absent physically, you will always be in relationship with them, energetically.

In the ELS Written Exercise for this chapter, you'll answer a series of questions about each of your parents, and the main issue you'll face if you fall in the Absent Category is feeling like it isn't necessary for you to complete this exercise, *because* your parent is absent. However, it's important to answer all of the questions as best you can, even if your answers are brief. If you were adopted or raised by someone other than your biological mother and father, or if you were raised by only one parent, answer a set of questions for each person who raised you *and* a set of questions for each of your biological parents.

THE CHALLENGING CATEGORY

If your relationship with one or both of your parents is characterized by abuse, trauma, neglect, or other intense difficulties, it falls into the Challenging Category. The main issue you may face in this category is not wanting to complete your ELS Written Exercise, because you don't want to "open up old wounds," especially if you've already done a lot of "work" on your relationship with your parents. However, the ELS Method will allow you to work on the issues you experience in relation to your parents in a completely new way, and the answers to your ELS Written Exercise for this chapter will provide you with crucial information for transforming your story in later stages—so it's very important to complete the exercise!

Another issue you may face in the Challenging Category is focusing so much on what your parents did *wrong* that you don't allow yourself to answer the questions about what they may have done *right*. I once spent thirty minutes trying to come up with a single positive thing to say about my dad. Deep down, part of me was afraid that if I acknowledged anything positive about him, I'd also be condoning everything that was negative about him, which would set me up to attract more of his negativity. But when I came to understand that acknowledging the positive aspects of my father's model actually made me feel *even freer* to disengage from the negative aspects of what he modeled, my resistance to acknowledging his positive attributes melted away.

So, if your relationship with one or both of your parents is in the Challenging Category, please understand that acknowledging anything positive about them—even the most basic things, like their having fed, clothed, and sheltered you—will provide you with a healthy way to connect with them so that you no longer feel an unconscious impulse to behave like them in *unhealthy* ways that don't serve you.

THE GREAT CATEGORY

If your relationship with one or both of your parents feels pretty good, it falls into the Great Category. In this category, you might also wonder, *Do I really need to do this ELS Written Exercise?* The answer is yes! There will still be subtle (and usually unconscious) ways in which their influence holds you back from achieving your dreams. Also, there will always be ways in which you can align even *more* powerfully with the positive aspects of what your parents modeled for you, and in doing so, you'll set yourself up for even greater success.

The main issue you'll likely face in the Great Category is feeling like you need to jump to your parents' defense, because you're not in the habit of seeing your parents as the source of any problems in your life. Even just entertaining the idea that your parents influenced you in some negative way will likely leave you feeling guilty—as if you're somehow betraying them just by reading this sentence. However, no parent is perfect, and no parental modeling is perfect, either. Accepting that truth, as you honestly explore the full spectrum of what your parents have modeled for you, will actually allow you to feel even *more* connected to your parents than you do right now.

2 Ways in Which You Respond to Parental Modeling

Your parents' model affects all aspects of your life—from how you handle finances to how you relate in love. And you respond to every pattern they modeled in one of two primary ways:

1. EMULATION RESPONSE

Emulation Response is when you directly copy your parents. As we discussed in the beginning of the chapter, you're predisposed to do this. You will feel the impulse to mimic your parents no matter which category your relationship with them falls into. However, the Emulation Response is usually strongest in the Absent Category, because behaving like your parent is the simplest and easiest way to feel connected to them. My client Mike recognized that he was emulating his father one day while sitting at a bar, drinking Johnny Walker and feeling sad about his failed acting career. He thought to himself, *What am I doing? I don't even like Johnny Walker.* But sitting at the bar, drinking Johnny Walker, and feeling sad about his failed acting career is exactly what his father did all the time before he passed away. Mike had unconsciously been looking for ways to stay connected to his father, and this ritual fit the bill. Seeing this Emulation Response in himself was Mike's first step toward breaking it.

2. REACTION RESPONSE

Reaction Response is when you intentionally create patterns of behavior *in reaction* to what your parents modeled. In other words, when you don't like what they modeled, you choose to do the exact opposite in ways that are often extreme. The problem with the Reaction Response is that it locks you into a polarized way of behaving and prevents you from seeing all the other options that are available to you. One of my clients promised herself when she was seven years old that she would never get divorced, like her parents did. She became so attached to this Reaction Response, that she didn't even allow herself to share her true feelings in her marriage for fear that it could lead to conflict, and then divorce. While the intention behind her Reaction Response was positive, it polarized her into an extreme way of behaving, that was actually preventing her from the very thing she wanted (a healthy, lasting marriage). Here also, seeing her own Reaction Response was the first step toward consciously choosing new patterns that were truly in her own best interest.

Whether you are emulating what your parents modeled for you or reacting against it, you have to ask yourself, *Does the way in which I'm responding to what my parents modeled for me support or inhibit the achievement of my dreams?* Answering this question is the first step toward consciously opting *out* of the aspects of your parental modeling that no longer serve you, and opting *into* the aspects that do.

For example, it was only after Mike answered this question for himself that he was able to opt *out* of his father's negative modeling (drinking Johnny Walker and feeling sad about his failed acting career) and opt *in* more powerfully to his father's positive modeling, which included pursuing his dream as an actor in the first place. Upgrading his own internal modeling allowed Mike to feel even more connected to his father, as if his success as an actor was an extension of the dream his father inspired in him, rather than a divergence from his father's model. This simple but profound reframe gave Mike the internal sense of freedom he needed to become a successful actor, and he now has dozens of IMDb credits on well-known film and TV productions to show for it.

5 Ways Parental Modeling Affects Your Dreams

Here's a deeper look into the ways in which your parental modeling affects you and your ability to realize your dreams:

1. **THEIR MODEL AFFECTS HOW YOU RELATE TO YOUR OWN NEEDS.**

    In order to feel like you deserve your dreams, you first have to feel that you deserve to have your basic needs met. If you went to bed hungry at night because your parents didn't meet your need to have enough food, the idea of going for your dreams might seem completely ridiculous. Whatever needs your parents failed to fulfill, you will likely struggle to fulfill for yourself, as an adult, simply because how you relate to your own needs is directly modeled after how your parents related to them. If you feel any resistance when completing your ELS Written Exercise, to identifying the needs your parents didn't meet for you, read the following message to yourself, as if it's from your parents:

    What you need matters to us. Expressing any feelings you have about how we may not have met all of your needs will not make us love you any less. On the contrary, it will help us feel even closer to you. We love you and we want to hear everything you need.

    This statement may be miles away from anything your parents have ever said to you in real life, but it's important for you to hear so that you feel free to complete your ELS Written Exercise honestly.

2. THEIR MODEL AFFECTS HOW YOU TALK TO YOURSELF.

The way your parents spoke to you is one of the most powerful aspects of their model, because it becomes how you speak to yourself, internally. If they spoke down to you every day, saying things like, "you're a loser," "you don't have what it takes," or "you're a spoiled brat," you will say those same things to yourself every day, too. And even if your parents only said *one* such negative thing to you, *one* time, it can still get stuck in your head, on repeat, for decades.

If your relationship with your parents falls into the Great Category, there's still a high likelihood that they said *something* negative to you, at some point, that has become woven into your internal dialogue—something you're telling yourself that makes it difficult for you to achieve your dreams. Even a well-intentioned statement, such as, "you'll always be my baby," can cause you to sabotage your own success, by making you feel like you will betray your parents if you grow up and become a financially independent adult.

3. THEIR MODEL AFFECTS HOW YOU DEAL WITH CHALLENGES.

You will always face challenges in the pursuit of your dreams, and the ELS Written Exercise in this chapter asks you to write about the challenges your parents faced and how they coped with them for a few reasons. If your parents avoided their challenges, or collapsed in the face of them, you will likely have a tendency to emulate that behavior. Conversely, if your parents faced challenges head on, you can draw on what they modeled for you as a source of strength and power.

Another reason to reflect on how your parents dealt with their own challenges, is to generate understanding for any negative ways they treated you *because* of the challenges they were facing; this understanding is not meant to condone any mistreatment from your parents or to invalidate your feelings about it, but rather, to untangle their failures as a parent from your own self-worth.

4. **THEIR MODEL AFFECTS HOW YOU EXPERIENCE LOVE AND RELATIONSHIPS.**

If manifesting a healthy romantic relationship is one of the results you listed in your ELS Intention, it's essential to take a good, honest look at what your parents modeled for you in that realm. If your parents modeled unhealthy—or even abusive—relationship dynamics, you may emulate the same patterns, or you may react against them by avoiding romantic relationships altogether—even if part of you dreams of creating a life-long, loving partnership.

If your parents modeled healthy relationship dynamics, emulation will serve you well (though there is always room for improvement!), but if your parents modeled unhealthy dynamics in love, the unconscious pull to follow in their footsteps will likely be an obstacle to achieving the kind of love you truly want. Either way, the ELS Method can help you upgrade your parental modeling in the realm of love and relationships.

5. **THEIR MODEL AFFECTS HOW YOU RELATE TO YOUR DREAMS, DIRECTLY.**

Your parents may have modeled any number of things when it comes to pursuing dreams. If you don't even know what one or both of your parents' dreams *are*, because they never shared them with you, that's significant. It means that they modeled feeling disconnected from their dreams, and you will likely feel the same. Even if you have an intellectual understanding that it's possible to achieve your dreams, you won't have a visceral imprint of what that feels like, because it was absent from your parents' model.

Another way your parents affect how you relate to your dreams directly is through specific things they said to you about your dreams. On one end of the spectrum, they may have told you that you could be, do, or have anything that you want. On the other end of the spectrum, they may have tried to "bring you back down to reality" whenever you shared a dream. They may have groomed you to make more practical choices, like to become a doctor or a lawyer, by telling you that it's not responsible—or even possible—to build a career doing what you love. Alternatively, they may have persuaded you to adopt one of their *own* unrealized dreams that they're trying to realize vicariously through you. If you have adopted a dream of theirs that isn't truly your own (which is different than authentically sharing a dream with them that they inspired in you), it's important to be honest with yourself.

Parent Freewrites

In your ELS Written Exercise for this chapter, you'll craft a Parent Freewrite for your mom and a Parent Freewrite for your dad (or whoever raised you). Parent Freewrites are five-sentence-long mini versions of your parents' stories. It's important to freewrite your parents' stories in the same way that you wrote your own: just put your pen down on paper and let them flow out, without planning what you'll write ahead of time. Later, you will distill these paragraphs down further, so keep them brief. As you freewrite, you'll gain insight into why your parents behaved in some of the ways they did, and you will likely feel greater understanding and empathy for them, as well. Remember, understanding your parents more doesn't excuse or condone any of their negative behaviors, but simply helps you realize that their negative behavior had nothing to do with you.

Parental Modeling Upgrade Statements

No matter what kind of relationship you have with your parents, there are powerful ways in which having been born to them uniquely prepared you to realize your dreams. To discover exactly *how* that's true, you'll identify your parents' negative qualities, habits, and patterns, and their positive qualities, habits, and patterns, as well. Then, you'll insert those responses into a template for your Parental Modeling Upgrade Statements, for both your mom and dad.

If your relationship with your parents is in the Great Category, you may experience resistance to naming their *negative* habits, qualities, and patterns. If your relationship with your parents is in the Challenging or Absent Category, you may experience resistance to naming their *positive* habits, qualities, and patterns. Regardless of the category of relationship you fall into with your parents, understanding how your parents have helped prepare you to realize your dreams will be incredibly liberating and will allow even more love to flow between you—so please answer all of the questions as best you can!

Path Skipping in Chapter 4

Exploring your relationship with your parents can bring up a lot of feelings and a lot of resistance; because of that, it's common to want to skip this chapter entirely. Don't! What you resist persists. Taking a good look at your relationship with your parents is a necessary step toward making deep and lasting changes in your life.

Any feelings of grief, sadness, hurt, or anger that arise during the process—regarding your parents or anyone else—will not last forever. And in the next chapter, you'll complete ELS Letters, an exercise that helps you to feel so much better regarding any past pain that has arisen. The deeper you let yourself drop into this chapter, and the more honestly you answer the questions, the better you will be able to provide yourself with relief in the next chapter.

Chapter 4 ELS Written Exercise

Before you begin, create a sacred, comfortable space to work. Turn off your devices and make sure you won't be interrupted for at least an hour. Read your ELS Intention aloud, and update it, if needed. Then, complete the following:

MOM QUESTIONS

1. What needs has your mom failed to fulfill for you?

2. What negative beliefs do you imagine you have about yourself as a result?

3. What needs of her own has she failed to fulfill for herself?

4. What negative things has your mom said to you?

5. Do you say any of those negative things to yourself?

6. What patterns has your mom modeled for you when it comes to coping with challenges?

7. In what ways do you emulate or react against what your mom modeled for you in coping with challenges?

8. If you're reacting against what your mom modeled for you in terms of coping with challenges, what other options might be available for you?

9. What has she explicitly said to you about coping with challenges (hers, yours, and/or in general)?

10. What patterns has your mom modeled for you when it comes to love and relationships?

11. In what ways do you emulate or react against what she modeled for you in love and relationships?

12. If you're reacting against what your mom modeled for you in love and relationships, what other options might be available for you?

13. What has your mom explicitly said to you about love and relationships (hers, yours, and/or in general)?

14. What has your mom modeled for you when it comes to how she relates to her dreams?

15. In what ways do you emulate or react against what she modeled about dreams?

16. If you're reacting against what your mom modeled for you about dreams, what other options might be available for you?

17. What has she explicitly said to you about realizing dreams (hers, yours, and/or in general)?

18. What are/were your mom's negative qualities, habits, and/or patterns?

19. In what ways do you emulate or react against her negative qualities, habits, and/or patterns?

20. In what ways do these negative qualities, habits, and/or patterns inhibit the realization of your dreams?

21. What positive qualities, habits, and/or patterns do you admire in your mom?

22. Which of these positive qualities, habits, and/or patterns could you benefit from emulating more strongly?

23. Complete your five-sentence Parent Freewrite about your mom.

24. Create the Parental Modeling Upgrade Statement for your mom.

   a. Which three negative qualities, habits or patterns (out of all your responses to #1 through #22 above) most get in the way of your dreams? Write your answers below.

   b. Which three positive qualities, habits or patterns (out of all your responses to #1 through #22 above) are most supportive of your dreams? Write your answers below.

   c. Complete the following template, using your answers from above:

   Being born to my mom has given me the opportunity to overcome _____, _____, and _____ (insert your answers from #24a) and to embrace what she modeled for me by in terms of _____, _____, and _____ (insert your answers from #24b).

DAD QUESTIONS

1. What needs has your dad failed to fulfill for you?

2. What negative beliefs do you imagine you have about yourself as a result?

3. What needs of his own has he failed to fulfill for himself?

4. What negative things has your dad said to you?

5. Do you say any of those negative things to yourself?

6. What patterns has your dad modeled for you when it comes to coping with challenges?

7. In what ways do you emulate or react against what your dad modeled for you in coping with challenges?

8. If you're reacting against what your dad modeled for you in terms of coping with challenges, what other options might be available for you?

9. What has he explicitly said to you about coping with challenges (his, yours, and/or in general)?

10. What patterns has your dad modeled for you when it comes to love and relationships?

11. In what ways do you emulate or react against what he modeled for you in love and relationships?

12. If you're reacting against what your dad modeled for you in love and relationships, what other options might be available for you?

13. What has your dad explicitly said to you about love and relationships (his, yours, and/or in general)?

14. What has your dad modeled for you when it comes to how he relates to his dreams?

15. In what ways do you emulate or react against what he modeled about dreams?

16. If you're reacting against what your dad modeled for you in terms of dreams, what other options might be available for you?

17. What has he explicitly said to you about realizing dreams (his, yours, and/or in general)?

18. What are/were your dad's negative qualities, habits, and/or patterns?

19. In what ways do you emulate or react against his negative qualities, habits, and/or patterns?

20. In what ways do these negative qualities, habits, and/or patterns inhibit the realization of your dreams?

21. What positive qualities, habits, and/or patterns do you admire in your dad?

22. Which of these positive qualities, habits, and/or patterns could you benefit from emulating more strongly?

23. Complete your five-sentence Parent Freewrite about your dad.

24. Create the Parental Modeling Upgrade Statement for your dad.

   a. Which three negative qualities, habits or patterns (out of all your responses to #1 through #22 above) most get in the way of your dreams? Write your answers below.

   b. Which three positive qualities, habits or patterns (out of all your responses to #1 through #22 above) are most supportive of your dreams? Write your answers below.

   c. Complete the following template, using your answers from above:

   Being born to my dad has given me the opportunity to overcome _____, _____, and _____ (insert your answers from #24a) and to embrace what he modeled for me by in terms of _____, _____, and _____ (insert your answers from #24b).

25. Afterwards, type your responses into your *ELS Written Exercises* document.

26. Have a trusted friend or writing partner provide you with feedback to ensure that you answered every question about each of your parents for this ELS Written Exercise.

27. Add any significant breakthroughs or results that you experience under the Breakthroughs and Results area of your *ELS Written Exercises* document.

in the bank

Visit www.TheELSResourceBank.com to download a printable version of the *Chapter 4 ELS Written Exercise,* which includes the instructions from this chapter that you'll need to complete your exercise.

Five

Resolving Unfinished Business with ELS Letters

Listening to and understanding our inner sufferings
will resolve most of the problems we encounter.

—THICH NHAT HANH

The purpose of this book is to lift your story to a higher level—one that makes you believe and achieve what previously felt impossible. In order for that to happen, you first have to make *space* for your dreams inside of your story.

If you're like most people on this planet, you're walking around with a lot more "unfinished business" than you realize—unfinished business that occupies your mind, eats up your creative energy, weighs down your story, and prevents you from having the mental freedom you need to focus on your dreams and bring them to life.

In this chapter you'll use an exercise that I created called Essential Life Story Letters (ELS Letters), which is the most powerful modality I've experienced for resolving feelings of anger and sadness that naturally arise when people have hurt you without making amends. ELS Letters are also the most powerful exercise I've experienced for freeing you to diverge from your parental modeling in any way that serves you and the realization of your Greatest Dreams.

Why ELS Letters Make You Feel So Good

There are a lot of other letter-writing techniques out there that involve writing your feelings to someone who has hurt you (without sending them the letter)—such as those described in *The Grief Recovery Handbook* by John W. James and Russell Friedman and *What You Can Feel, You Can Heal* by John Gray. Abraham Lincoln even swore by writing his feelings of anger in letters to people who had wronged him, without ever sending them.

The problem with writing such letters however, is that they make you feel better only for a time—it's like taking the top off a tea kettle without removing it from the stove. The pressure builds right back up again. In John Grey's book, he shared that he and his wife had to write hundreds of these "Love Letters" to each other; and I remember wondering, *If they work so well, why do you have to keep rewriting them?*

What sets ELS Letters apart from these other letter writing techniques is that they not only provide you with a way to express what you need to say to someone who has hurt you, but they also provide you with a way to simulate the experience of receiving a letter of apology *back* from the other person—without having to interact with them in real life.

You've probably seen countless memes on social media about how important forgiveness is, and that it's for *your benefit* not the other person's. However, advice about forgiveness can be frustrating to hear, because you already know that forgiveness is good for you. It just isn't easy! You can't simply snap your fingers and forgive someone who has seriously wronged you. And there's actually a *good reason* you can't forgive the other person: you need amends from them first. The truth is, just because someone is unable or unwilling to give you what you need, doesn't mean you don't need it.

Receiving an incredibly comprehensive and customized apology for every single thing someone has done to hurt you—through ELS Letters—can feel just as real, powerful, healing, and cathartic as hearing it from the other person in real life. After receiving that apology, your system will literally dump all of the old feelings of hurt and anger, because you will finally have received what you needed. And those negative feelings won't build back up again either, so you'll only need to write these letters once.

After completing ELS Letters, I've heard clients say, "I feel twenty pounds lighter," and "I feel twenty years younger." They've said, "I feel good about things that I've felt terrible about my whole life," and "I never thought I could feel compassion for this person, but I do." My clients have successfully used these letters to get over their exes (I actually invented ELS Letters to help me get over an ex and it worked like a charm), save their marriages, and forgive friends and family members who have betrayed or abandoned them. They've used ELS Letters to dissolve the impulse to emulate their parents in negative ways, resolve unfinished business with loved ones who have passed away, stop blaming themselves for things that weren't their fault, renew their faith in Source, and stop projecting pain from past relationships onto their current ones.

And because ELS Letters allow you to receive the validation, amends, and appreciation you deserve, they also strengthen your boundaries, improve your self-worth, and inspire others to treat you better. One of the most beautiful things about ELS Letters is that they also allow you to feel forgiveness toward the other person naturally, without even having to try. As an added bonus—and this may seem like some sort of sorcery, but it's actually a normal part of the process—people frequently tell me that the person they completed ELS Letters with reached out to them afterwards and apologized for things they've never apologized for before, saying things that seem to have come straight out of their ELS Letters—so don't be surprised when that happens!

And finally, because ELS Letters work with the inherent wisdom of your own emotions, you don't have to worry that they'll ruin a relationship with someone you love or bring you closer to someone you want to let go of—they always result in the healthiest, best, and most loving outcome for you.

Your ELS Letters List

You'll begin your ELS Written Exercise for this chapter by making a list of the people with whom you need to write ELS Letters. You can write ELS Letters with people you cherish and want to keep in your life, as well as with people you wouldn't mind seeing fall off the face of the Earth.

There are three relationships that you *must* complete ELS Letters with before you move onto the next chapter: each of your parents and one romantic partner, past or present, so add them to your list first. Then, add anyone that you feel hurt by, wronged by, upset with, or confused about. You can write ELS Letters with literally anyone—dead or alive—including your parents, guardians, ex-lovers, current partners, siblings, relatives, friends, mentors, yourself, Source, and even entire groups or institutions that you feel wronged by (such as the Catholic Church, the Internal Revenue Service, or the entertainment business).

You can also reflect on your 5-Page Freewrite to see if there is anyone else that you have unfinished business with, and add them to your ELS Letters List. You can put as many people as you want on your ELS Letters List—the more you write, the better you will feel! Try to keep your ELS Letters List in an order where the relationships that hold you back the *most* from realizing your dreams are at the top, after your parents and partner. But don't worry about getting the order of the people on your ELS Letters List "perfect" before you begin; you can always adjust the order as you go.

Instructions for Creating the Expression Letter

When completing ELS Letters with someone, you will write two letters: an Expression Letter *to* the other person AND a Response Letter *from* them. You'll begin with your Expression Letter, where you'll write *by hand* all of your feelings toward the other person in the following four emotional categories: anger, sadness, regret, and appreciation—*in that order*. The order is important, because your emotions are layered, and heavier emotions like hatred and anger are sitting on top of lighter emotions like love and appreciation (that's why it's so hard to feel the love that you have for someone when you're angry at them).

1. **WRITE TO THE OTHER PERSON'S HIGHER SELF.**

   Before you begin, you'll imagine that you'll be writing to the other person's higher self—the version of them who has suddenly become enlightened and is ready to hear *all* of your feelings—no matter how intense—without getting upset, triggered, or defensive. The other person's higher self *wants* to hear *all* of your feelings, because they're ready to take full responsibility for their own behavior, so there is no need to feel guilty about expressing too many heavy emotions to them! Writing to the other person in this way allows you to fully express yourself without censorship, which is necessary for ELS Letters to work.

2. **BE COMPREHENSIVE!**

   The more feelings you express about things you need the other person to take responsibility for, the better you will feel in the end. Your Expression Letter should be however long it needs to be (I've seen some as long as ten pages), because while "essential" is the name of the game with most of the ELS Method, "comprehensive" is the name of the game with ELS Letters. If you leave a grievance out of your Expression Letter, it cannot be addressed in the Response Letter, so you'll have to continue carrying it around.

Before considering any Expression Letter complete, ask yourself, *Is there anything else the other person did, didn't do, said or didn't say that any part of me needs to express feelings about?* Often, the feelings you need to express that hold the greatest potential to change your life come out after asking yourself that question.

3. **DON'T WORRY ABOUT CHRONOLOGICAL ORDER OR THE ORDER OF EMOTIONS.**

While chronological order is important in your ELS itself, it doesn't matter at all in your ELS Letters. Your feelings about experiences in your relationship with other people will often arise out of chronological order, and that's totally fine! You can express anger about something someone did to you when you were a baby right after you express anger about what they did to you last week. What's most important when writing ELS Letters is that you get *all* of your feelings out. Also, it's common, after you've moved from one emotional category to the next, for more feelings to arise that belong in the *previous* category. That's fine, too. For example, if you feel a spike of anger after you've moved onto sadness, just write your feelings of anger in the sadness section and then return to expressing the rest of your sadness.

4. **GIVE ALL ASPECTS OF YOURSELF A VOICE.**

Sometimes, when you're writing your Expression Letter, you'll start to write feelings of anger about something, and then another part of you will question that anger. For example, you might write, *I hate you for breaking up with me.* And then another part of you might think, *But I appreciate that they broke up with me, because now I understand that we're not compatible.* When you notice this kind of internal debate, it's evidence that different parts of you feel differently, and they both need to be given a voice! In this case, you would leave the first statement in the anger category, and move the second statement into the appreciation category. You don't have to figure out which part is right or wrong. Simply ensuring that each part of you feels heard will lead to inner peace.

5. DON'T MAKE EXCUSES FOR THE OTHER PERSON!

As I mentioned in the beginning of this chapter, ELS Letters will naturally lead you to feel understanding, empathy, and forgiveness towards the other person. When feelings of forgiveness arise while writing your Expression Letter (before crafting your Response Letter), it's common to want to write statements that excuse the other person's behavior, like, *You probably didn't know any better.* However, writing excuses limits the other person's ability to take full responsibility for their behavior in the Response Letter—so don't do it! Similarly, when expressing regrets to the other person in your Expression Letter, don't apologize for anything you didn't actually say or do to them. For example, avoid statements like, *I'm sorry you had such a hard life.* Doing so is a subtle way to provide the other person with an "out" that prevents them from taking full responsibility for their own behavior.

6. EXPRESS YOUR ANGER.

Begin your Expression Letter by writing your feelings of anger or hatred about anything the other person did to you, said to you, or *didn't* do or say to you that you *needed* them to. For example: *I hate you for cheating on me* (something they did); *I hate you for calling me a bitch* (something they said); *I hate you for not returning my calls* (something they didn't do); and *I hate you for NOT telling me I was beautiful* (something they didn't say). It's very important that most of your statements begin with the words *I feel angry that you _____ or I hate you for _____.* Leading with your feelings keeps you grounded in the power of your own emotional experience. However, feel free to sprinkle in some statements that *don't* begin with *I feel,* such as *Fuck you, I hate you,* or *You fucking asshole,* as doing so will lend authenticity to your Expression Letter. Swear as much as you want, because it's natural for intense feelings of hatred and anger to come out that way. And don't be surprised if your Expression Letter has significantly more anger than any other emotion—that's very common and perfectly okay. You'll know when you've gotten to the bottom of your old, buried anger when sadness starts to arise.

7. **EXPRESS YOUR SADNESS.**

Next, you'll express your feelings of sadness or hurt about anything the other person did to you, said to you, or *didn't* do or say to you that you needed them to. Be sure here, too, to lead with your emotions, beginning most statements with *I feel sad that* _____ or *I feel hurt because you* _____. For example: *I'm sad that you left me* (something they did); *I'm sad that you told me you didn't love me anymore* (something they said); *I'm sad that you've never met my children* (something they didn't do); and *I'm sad that you never told me you were proud of me* (something they didn't say). It's natural to feel hurt or sad about many of the same things you already expressed anger about, but you don't have to name those things again in this category, because expressions of anger and sadness will be treated the same way in the Response Letter.

8. **EXPRESS YOUR REGRETS.**

After expressing your sadness, you can apologize for anything that *you* did, said, didn't do, or didn't say to the other person that is weighing you. If the person you're writing your Expression Letter to was abusive, you may not have anything to apologize for, and that's completely fine. However, you may need to write a statement like, *I regret that I didn't feel strong enough to hold you accountable for your actions.* Conversely, if you played the role of abuser in any of your relationships, you may have a lot you need to apologize for, and that's okay too. Just have love and compassion for yourself as you take responsibility for your own behavior, because doing so takes a lot of courage.

9. **EXPRESS YOUR APPRECIATION.**

The final category of emotion is appreciation. In the Appreciation section of your Expression Letter, you'll write everything you love and appreciate about the other person. You'll find that it's much easier to get in touch with appreciation after you've released the heavier feelings that are sitting on top of it—especially in relationships where a lot of bad was mixed with the good. If you find that you have little or nothing to say in this category, as is often the case in an Expression Letter with someone who has seriously wronged you, that's completely fine too—just leave it blank.

10. **TYPE UP YOUR EXPRESSION LETTER.**

After writing your Expression Letter by hand, you'll type it word-for-word into a document titled *ELS Letters with (the name of the person)*. Typing your Expression Letter is essential for making any necessary changes and also for crafting your Response Letter.

11. **REMOVE STATEMENTS THAT BELONG IN A DIFFERENT EXPRESSION LETTER.**

When writing an Expression Letter, it's common to sometimes express your feelings about things that aren't actually the other person's responsibility—things that belong in an Expression Letter to someone else. For example, when working on an Expression Letter to your mom, you might write, *I'm angry that Dad was so abusive.* While it *would* be appropriate to express anger toward your mom for not protecting you from his abuse (*I'm angry that you didn't protect me from Dad.*), your feelings about your father's abuse should be saved for an Expression Letter with *him*. It's important to include statements in your Expression Letter about *only* things for which the person you're writing to needs to take responsibility.

12. ELABORATE ON GENERAL AND VAGUE STATEMENTS.

In your Expression Letter, you'll notice general statements like, *I'm angry at you for being abusive,* and they're a great way to describe overarching patterns. But it's important to follow such general statements with specific details, such as, *I'm angry at you for slapping me* and *I'm angry at you for calling me stupid.* Similarly, if a vague statement comes out in your Expression Letter, such as, *I hate what you did to me in high school,* you would need to add a statement immediately following it that describes exactly what transpired between you and the other person, as in, *I hate that you always told me to go away when your friends came over.* The more specific you are in your Expression Letter, the more resolution your Response Letter will bring.

After writing your Expression Letter, you will feel a sense of lightness and relief. And you will feel even greater lightness and relief after crafting your Response Letter. Between now and then, you'll be in what I call the "in-between," where you will see evidence of how your relationship dynamics with the other person are already changing, even if only energetically. And, at the same time, because you will not have yet received what you need from the other person in response, you will still feel unresolved. This duality is a normal part of the process, and it's temporary. After completing your Response Letter, and having a trusted friend or writing partner read it to you, you will experience the signature cathartic release that ELS Letters always bring.

Instructions for Crafting the Response Letter

Your Response Letter is where you'll receive the *ideal* response from your *ideal* version of the other person (or, the other person's higher self).

You will create this letter directly from your typed-up Expression Letter by copying it into a new document and then converting it line-by-line according to the instructions below:

1. **ADD THE OPENING MESSAGE TO THE TOP.**

   Every Response Letter should begin with: *Thank you for sharing all of your feelings with me. There are many things that I need to apologize to you for.* This opening conveys that the other person is grateful for having heard everything you shared with them in the Expression Letter; it also prepares you to receive the apologies you're about to hear.

2. **USE THE RIGHT TENSE TO PROVIDE HOPE FOR CHANGE.**

   The only time grammar is significant when using the ELS Method is when it impacts the transformational power of your writing, and this is one of those times. Your Response Letter is best written using present perfect tense. That means, when you're converting a sentence like, *I hate you for being so selfish,* you would write, *I'm sorry I **have been** so selfish,* instead of, *I'm sorry I **am** so selfish.* This distinction is important because if you write, *I'm sorry I **am** so selfish,* there's no room for this pattern to change *and* it lacks the acknowledgement of *past* behavior. Remember, you're writing on behalf of the version of this person who has suddenly become enlightened, and that person's poor behavior would not continue. You can also add a statement of planned action, like, *I'm going to get the help that I need so that from now on, I can be there for you as you need me to be, and make sure that our relationship feels balanced and reciprocal.*

3. **CONVERT STATEMENTS OF ANGER INTO APOLOGIES.**

   Everything you expressed anger about in your Expression Letter will become an apology in the Response Letter. For example, if you wrote in your Expression Letter, *I hate you for cheating on me*, change that sentence to read, *I'm sorry for cheating on you*. Continue converting each statement of anger line-by-line in this way, until each has become an apology. Delete any statements that don't begin with *I feel*, such as *Fuck you* and *Screw you* from the Response Letter (those statements were important to help you release your anger, but they do not require a response). Additionally, it's important to honor the distinction between who someone inherently *is* and how they *behave*. So if you wrote a statement in your Expression Letter like, *I hate you for being an asshole,* you would convert that into, *I'm sorry for **acting like** an asshole,* instead of, *I'm sorry for **being** an asshole,* because the former statement allows room for change in your ideal version of the other person.

4. **CONVERT STATEMENTS OF SADNESS INTO APOLOGIES.**

    Everything you expressed sadness about in your Expression Letter will also become an apology in the Response Letter. For example, if you wrote in your Expression Letter, *I'm sad that you never even said goodbye,* change that sentence to read, *I am so sorry that I never even said goodbye.* If there are any statements of sadness that speak to something you already expressed anger for (and thus, converted into an apology in the previous section), just delete that sentence, because it has already been addressed.

5. **CONVERT STATEMENTS OF REGRET INTO FORGIVENESS.**

    Everything that you expressed regret about, or apologized for, in your Expression Letter, will become a statement of forgiveness from the other person in your Response Letter. For example, if you wrote in your Expression Letter, *I'm sorry I didn't speak up about how I really felt,* change it to read, *I forgive you for not speaking up about how you really felt.* You can also add statements of understanding from the other person, such as, *I know I didn't make it easy for you to share your feelings with me.* If you apologized to the other person for many things in your Expression Letter, consider using the following message in your Response Letter to address all of your apologies at once: *I appreciate all of the things you apologized for. But please know that all is forgiven. The truth is, if I'd been there for you in the ways you needed me to be, none of those things that you apologized for would have happened in the first place.*

6. **WRITE STATEMENTS OF APPRECIATION FROM SCRATCH.**

Since you're crafting your Response Letter directly from a copy of your Expression Letter, it will initially include the statements of appreciation that you wrote toward the other person. Delete those statements and replace them with the following message: *Thank you for sharing everything you love and appreciate about me—it means so much. Now I'd like to express everything that I love and appreciate about you, too.* Then write from scratch everything you'd like to hear the other person express love and appreciation to *you* for. For example, you may want to write, *You're such an incredibly smart, beautiful, talented, and loving person. You're the most amazing person I've ever known, and I'm so lucky to have gotten to know you.* Even if you didn't express appreciation toward the other person in your Expression Letter, it's still important that you receive appreciation from *them* in your Response Letter.

7. **ADD STATEMENTS OF EMPHASIS.**

The Response Letter will primarily consist of statements of apology. However, it's important to periodically break up apologies with brief statements of emphasis, where it feels natural, such as, *That was really messed up; That was really fucked up; That was beyond wrong; I never should have done that to you in a million years;* or

That was the biggest mistake of my life. Such statements prevent your Response Letter from sounding mechanical and insincere, and vastly increase its transformational impact by adding depth and authenticity. However, it's important to avoid adding statements like, *I'm such a terrible person* or *I am so disgusting,* because these are derogatory statements about who the other person inherently *is* rather than addressing their problematic *behavior.*

8. **ADD A STATEMENT ACKNOWLEDGING THAT AN APOLOGY ISN'T ENOUGH.**

    It may sound counterintuitive to acknowledge in your Response Letter that an apology can never undo the harm that the other person caused you, since the Response Letter usually does just that. However, if you include the following acknowledgement, it will increase your openness to receiving the apologies: *I know a mere apology can never undo the harm that I have caused you, but I need you to know how truly sorry I am.* It's important to add this message to your Response Letter at least once, immediately before or after they apologize for their behavior that hurt you the most, such as abandoning you, or failing you in some other traumatic way.

9. **ADD STATEMENTS ABOUT HOW YOU *SHOULD* HAVE BEEN TREATED.**

    Wherever it feels important, follow an apology with a sentence about how you would have ideally liked the other person to have behaved, instead. For example, you can follow a statement like, *I'm sorry I never complimented you,* with, *I should have told you how smart, funny, and beautiful you are every day, because it's true.* You can follow, *I'm sorry I was never there for you,* with, *I should have been there every day, because I love you.* Remember that the Response Letter is from your *ideal* version of the other person, so don't hold back in describing how they would have ideally treated you.

10.   ADD THE IT-WASN'T-YOUR-FAULT MESSAGE.

Whenever you have blamed yourself for things that were the *other person's* responsibility, add a clear message to your Response Letter about how their behavior was not your fault. For example, follow a statement like, *I'm so sorry that I hit you,* with something like, *I know you already know this, but I need you to know that I know it now too—it was not your fault. There's nothing that you could've ever done that would've warranted my hitting you. I'm so sorry for taking my pain and anger out on you with violence.* Even if you're not consciously blaming yourself for the other person's behavior, it's important to include a message like this whenever you were abused, neglected, or betrayed in any way.

11.   PROVIDE DEEPER UNDERSTANDING.

When you've been seriously hurt by someone, it's common to be plagued by the following question: *Why did this person treat me this way?* Without knowing the answer to that question, it's difficult—maybe even impossible—to forgive the grievance. The truth is, most people hurt you for fairly simple reasons. One of the most common being that they're in pain, and are taking it out on you. If you feel like that's the case, add the following message to your Response Letter: *I say this not as an excuse, but just for you to understand—I only treated you in such hurtful ways because I was hurting so badly inside myself. But that was my problem, not yours. And I'm sorry for not getting the help I needed, so that I could treat you with the love, kindness, and respect that you deserve.* Another reason someone may hurt you is that they're afraid of losing you, so they're trying to push you away before *you* leave *them.* If you feel like that's the case, add the following message to your Response Letter: *I say this not as an excuse, but just for you to understand—I only treated you in such hurtful ways because deep down, I felt like I wasn't good enough for you. I was so afraid of losing you that I tried to push you away before you could leave me. But I want you to know that I'm going to get the help I need so that I can be there for you and love and respect you, as you deserve, from now on.*

12. **DON'T LET THE RESPONSE LETTER BECOME FOCUSED ON** *THEIR* **NEEDS.**

Avoid adding statements to the Response Letter that make the letter about *their* needs, instead of yours. For example, never add a statement like, *I'm so ashamed of how I treated you, please forgive me,* because such a statement is a bid for you to assuage the other person's guilt. It's important for the other person to never ask you for forgiveness—in any way—in your Response Letter. The Response Letter is written from your ideal version of the other person—a fully mature, self-responsible adult who doesn't need anything from you in return for the amends they're making. If you're worried that focusing exclusively on your own needs will make you a narcissist, please know that the opposite is actually true. When the other person takes full responsibility for their behavior, you will naturally feel more understanding, empathy, and forgiveness, as well as clarity about your own responsibility in the relationship dynamic.

Reading ELS Letters

Writing your ELS Letters is transformational on its own, but having a trusted friend or writing partner read your Response Letter to you aloud takes the experience to a whole new level of catharsis. It's magical how real it feels when someone steps into the role of the person you need amends from. I recommend having someone read the Response Letter to you over the phone, as opposed to in person, because you'll feel more comfortable in your own space where you won't have to worry about what you look like if you cry (which is very common when experiencing such a cathartic release).

Your partner should read the Response Letter to you at a slow pace, taking long pauses after significant apologies, so you can really take them in. It's crucial that the only thing your reading partner says to you after reading your Response Letter is something like, "You did such a great job on these letters." Warm encouragement is all you should hear. Please warn your reading partner ahead of time that they should *not*—under any circumstances—convey empathy, understanding, or (worst-of-all) excuses for the person you just completed ELS Letters with.

You'll be in a very vulnerable place after hearing your Response Letter, and it's best to minimize talking and ideally, spend a couple hours alone resting or taking a nap. Your entire system will be releasing old emotions and reorganizing itself around what you just heard.

If you're completing ELS Letters on your own, record yourself reading your Response Letter aloud, and then listen to the recording. Being able to hear the reading will magnify your results.

And remember, ELS Letters are NOT to be shared with the person you wrote them with; they are not a forum for dialogue. ELS Letters are designed only to facilitate your own internal transformation.

in the bank Visit www.TheELSResourceBank.com and download *Guidelines for Reading ELS Letters,* which is a handout that you can give to your reading partner ahead of time.

On Parent Letters

Parent Letters, or ELS Letters with your parents or whoever raised you, are written in the same way as ELS Letters with anyone else and they bring the same benefits. However, there are important additions that you need to make to your Parent Letters that bring the added benefit of completing the work you began in chapter 4, of upgrading your internal parental modeling.

No matter which category of relationship you fall into with your parents—the Absent Category, the Challenging Category, or the Great Category—Parent Letters will allow you to feel more respected, loved, and valued by your parents, while at the same time, allowing you to feel more understanding, empathy, and forgiveness toward them.

That said, the greatest benefit of Parent Letters, in my opinion, is that they provide you with a simple way of creating an internal sense of permission to differentiate yourself from your parents, to break free from the negative impact of anything they modeled for you, or didn't model for you that you needed them to. For example, if your parents were completely disconnected from their own creativity and you are extremely creative, you'll struggle to express your creativity. You may even tell yourself that you're not creative, especially if they didn't praise you for it.

Under those circumstances, everyone in the world could tell you that you're super creative and that you should make a living from your art, but—crazy as it might sound—part of you would never believe it, because you never heard it directly from your parents. When you hear your parents apologize in your Parent Response Letters, for not having modeled connection to their creativity and for not having praised your own, and when you hear them tell you how creative you truly are and how, *Of course you should make a living out of your art*, the information sticks. The positive things that your parents say to you, by proxy, through your Parent Letters are naturally and automatically absorbed by your system—they become the new things you say to yourself, internally.

The additions you need to make to your Parent Letters to effectively upgrade your parental modeling in the way I'm describing, include: revisiting your ELS Written Exercise for chapter 4, using the "Negative Modeling Disengagement Formula," reinforcing your parent's positive modeling, and adding praise and encouragement from your parents to go for your Greatest Dreams.

in the bank

You can visit www.TheELSResourceBank.com and download *Additional Parent Letter Instructions*, for detailed guidance on how to make these additions to ELS Letters with your parents.

Path Skipping in Chapter 5

Because of how transformative ELS Letters are, you'll likely experience more resistance in this stage of the process than in any other. The most detrimental way to skip off the path in this chapter is to not complete ELS Letters with both of your parents and one romantic partner before moving on to the next chapter.

Still, you may come up with a whole host of reasons to avoid writing these three important sets of ELS Letters. One of my clients put up a big fight in this stage of the process, because he didn't want to write ELS Letters with his ex-girlfriend, with whom he'd had an extremely tumultuous relationship. He gave me many reasons why he shouldn't complete this exercise, the strongest being that his pain wasn't a "bad" thing and that he actually needed it in his work as an actor.

I let him know that he was right, his pain *isn't* a bad thing, and that he would always be able to draw on it in his work. I told him that completing ELS Letters would actually help him draw on his pain even *more* effectively, because that pain would no longer be dominating his daily thoughts, so he could revisit those painful memories without the fear of getting stuck in them. However, I told him that the most important reason for him to complete ELS Letters with ex was because she was occupying his mind all the time, and therefore, robbing him of the mental space that he needed to focus on his dreams. After a lively 45-minute debate, he agreed, and he had such a transformational experience with this set of ELS Letters that he manifested the best relationship he'd ever had only two weeks later.

in the bank

If you feel stalled or stuck when writing ELS Letters, visit www.TheELSResourceBank.com and download *Troubleshooting ELS Letters*. In it, you will find a targeted list of what could be getting in the way and how to overcome it.

Chapter 5 ELS Written Exercise

Please understand that these instructions are based on thousands of hours of trials. For optimal results, *please follow the instructions to the letter.* Before you begin, create a sacred, comfortable space to work. Turn off your devices and make sure you won't be interrupted. Read your ELS Intention aloud, and update it, if needed. Then, complete the following:

1. Write your ELS Letters List. Start with both of your parents and one romantic partner (past or present), and then add everyone with whom you have unfinished business, in order of the negative impact they have on your dreams (greatest impact first).

2. Write an Expression Letter by hand to the first person on your ELS Letters List, following the Instructions for Creating The Expression Letter.

3. Create your Response Letter, following the Instructions for Crafting Your Response Letter.

4. Have a trusted friend or writing partner review your ELS Letters to make sure that you followed the instructions and then read your Response Letter to you aloud, as if they are the person it is from. If you can't have someone else read to you, record yourself reading the Response Letter aloud and then listen to the recording.

5. Record any breakthroughs or results that you experience while completing any set of ELS Letters in your *ELS Written Exercises* document in the Breakthroughs and Results area, and make sure you begin by writing the date you experienced the breakthrough or result.

6. Choose the next person on your ELS Letters List and complete steps two through five until you've written a set of ELS Letters for at least the top three people on your ELS Letters List before moving on to chapter 6 (you will be prompted later in the book to come back and complete more ELS Letters, as needed).

in the bank

Visit www.TheELSResourceBank.com to download a printable version of the *Chapter 5 ELS Written Exercise,* which includes the instructions from this chapter that you'll need to complete your exercise.}

Six

Identifying Your Story Core

The secret of change is to focus all of your energy,
not on fighting the old, but on building the new.

— SOCRATES

If you were to read your 5-Page Freewrite now, you would feel very different about it than you did when you first wrote it. The ELS Letters have opened up a significant amount of space in both your story and your psyche, and even though that opening is incredibly positive, it leaves you with a void that your mind wants to fill. But what will you fill the space with?

In this chapter, you'll take the first steps toward consciously filling this newfound space in your mind and story with experiences and emotions that make you a magnet for your Greatest Dreams. As I mentioned in chapter 3, your old story is likely more negative than positive, and you likely left a lot of positive experiences and relationships *out* of your 5-Page Freewrite. In this chapter, you'll begin balancing the "dark" and "light" aspects of your story by identifying the missing positive pieces that need to be integrated into your dominant narrative. These positive life experiences will come to play a more prominent role in the new version of your story, and one of these experiences will be the gravitational center of your Essential Life Story, as your Story Core.

The Purpose of Your Story Core

The root of the word courage is *Cor,* which means "heart" in Latin. That's fitting, because your Story *Core* is a positive, empowering memory that is very dear to your heart; and it takes courage to claim it and make it the central experience of your life. Your Story Core will set the vibrational tone of your new story, and everything else will be organized around it.

In your ELS Written Exercise for this chapter, you'll brainstorm potential Story Core candidates, freewrite about a couple of them (including the lessons you learned from each experience and the meaning you assign to it), and then select the freewrite that feels most inspiring to sit at the heart of your ELS. The positive experience you choose as your Story Core can literally be *any* positive experience—such as a trip abroad, your first kiss, an enlightening conversation, or a memory of being on stage—as long as it's the one memory that lights you up the *most.*

In the film *The Prisoner of Azkaban*, Harry Potter's teacher, Professor Lupin tells his class how to cast a spell to fight off Dementors, dark creatures that can make you feel cold, lose hope, and literally suck the life out of you. Lupin says, "The spell I'm going to try and teach you is called a Patronus charm... a Patronus is a kind of positive force... it works something like a shield... but in order for it to work, you need to think of a memory. Not just any memory, a very happy memory, a very powerful memory."

After Harry tries the spell and fails the first time, Professor Lupin asks Harry which memory he chose. Harry tells the professor that he chose the memory of the first time he rode a broom. Professor Lupin responds that the memory isn't good enough. So Harry tries again. This time he thinks of a memory of his parents' faces when they were talking to him—it was the happiest he had ever been—and when he thinks of *that* memory, Harry is successful in casting the spell. Later, when Harry teaches his friends to cast the same spell, he tells them, "Make it a powerful memory—the happiest you can remember. Allow it to fill you up."

Just like Dementors, the "dark" experiences in your story can make you feel cold, hopeless, and empty. The purpose of creating a Patronus in the world of Harry Potter is similar to the purpose of creating a Story Core in the ELS Method: to protect you from being overtaken by darkness. That said, your Story Core and a Patronus have an important difference: the goal of your Story Core is *not* to completely drive away the darkness.

Upon hearing that your Story Core is supposed to be a positive experience, you might feel a sudden urge to simply cut out every dark experience from your 5-Page Freewrite, but I strongly advise against that. The intention of your Story Core is *not* to create a surface-level fix, and it's not meant to dismiss the heaviness in your story. It's actually very important to have both dark and light in your story. The dark aspects of your story will always exist inside of you, and removing them from your written story will only prevent you from bringing them into balance with the light.

A common strategy in New Age thinking is to "focus only on the positive." The truth is that while focusing primarily on the positive will lead you to attract *more* positive experiences in your life, being dismissive of your negative experiences is counter-productive. The parts of you that struggled through hardships will feel dishonored, which will lead to internal conflict. When you include the negative aspects of your story—correctly balanced with the positive—you satisfy both aspects of yourself and it becomes even easier to focus on the positive.

Think of the darkness, or the negative parts of your story, as bad guys in a movie. Bad guys are essential in movies, because they provide good guys with the opportunity to develop strength and triumph over evil. But if the bad guys are too prominent, the audience will walk away cynical and depressed, instead of uplifted and inspired. Imagine for a moment how different you would feel after watching *Harry Potter* if Voldemort had twice as much screen time as Harry.

The duration of time you spend focusing on negative experiences in your story matters. It's the biggest determining factor in how your story ultimately makes you feel.

Keira's Story Core

My client Keira is a two-time cancer survivor. When we first got to this chapter, she immediately assumed her Story Core would be about surviving cancer. After all, that was the most important part of her story. Without having survived cancer, she literally wouldn't be alive. However, when I told her that she needed to choose a *positive experience* as her Story Core, she couldn't help but pause and question everything she thought she knew about herself.

Keira's entire identity had been built around beating cancer—a major life victory. And here I was, providing her with instructions that required her to make a *different choice* about what was most important in her story—a choice that would revolutionize her identity. She acknowledged that if she was honest with herself, the actual process of beating cancer wasn't a memory that she wanted to focus on. I let her know that even though she needed to choose a different, more positive memory than beating cancer for her Story Core, her survival experience would still *be* in her ELS—it just would no longer dominate the story and define who she is.

Keira's story perfectly illustrates the importance of having a positive memory as your Story Core. As long as the central focus of Keira's story was about being a survivor, she would continue to attract situations that required her to struggle to *survive*. But she didn't want to stay stuck in survivor mode. Keira said, "What I really want is to *thrive*." As soon as she said that out loud, a memory arose in her mind.

It was her earliest memory—one she didn't think of very often. She was a little baby in her crib, and she felt God shine down upon her and wrap her up in a blanket of white light. She felt protected, taken care of, and like everything was going to be okay. Recalling this memory and describing it to me felt amazing to Keira.

After reconnecting to this beautiful memory, Keira updated her ELS Intention to include *thriving* as one of the results she wanted through the process, and then she crafted this memory into her Story Core. Afterwards, she felt close to the Divine every day. When new challenges arose, she felt safer, more trusting, and like God was taking care of her. She no longer felt like she had to just "get by," as she had when "survival" was the center of her story. She said, "That image of being in the crib is integrated into me now, the essence is alive for me. I don't have to conjure it up or anything—it's with me all the time."

Remembering a powerfully positive memory will always make you feel good; but integrating it properly into your story will remove that memory from a forgotten shelf in your mind, and make it the star of your story, where it will never get lost in the shadows of your mind again.

Additional Benefits of Your Story Core

The most important benefit of your Story Core is the one we already discussed: it protects you from being overtaken by darkness. But your Story Core also provides you with the following additional benefits.

1. YOUR STORY CORE PROVIDES YOUR ELS WITH STRUCTURE AND FOCUS.

Centering your ELS around a core event provides your story with a clear beginning, middle, and end. When you assemble your ELS (in chapter 9), the beginning will consist of everything leading up to your Story Core, the middle will consist of your Story Core, and the ending will consist of everything that follows. Your Story Core will become the warm, glowing center of your story, the beating heart, and it will bring light to all the other parts of your story.

2. **YOUR STORY CORE HELPS YOU INTEGRATE YOUR HERO'S JOURNEY.**

In the preface of this book, I talked about how Joseph Campbell's book *The Hero with a Thousand Faces* was an inspiration for the ELS Method. Campbell says that every hero's journey includes the same steps—the most important and difficult of which is the final one: integrating what you've learned and sharing it with others. I have found it to be profoundly true that you have to integrate what you've learned from powerful experiences in order to complete the hero's journey. After returning home from the jungle, I didn't know *how* to integrate and complete my journey. Crafting my Story Core, 10 years later, was the answer: it allowed me to integrate what I had learned so that I could access the emotional power and wisdom from my time in the Amazon, every day.

3. **YOUR STORY CORE CLARIFIES YOUR PURPOSE.**

Knowing, pursuing, and fulfilling your purpose is an essential human need. Often, the idea of naming or clarifying your purpose can feel stressful, and bring with it a lot of pressure. But your true purpose will always provide you with a sense of joy, inspiration, and fulfillment, and since your Story Core involves an experience where you were feeling those same emotions, your Story Core will reveal your purpose to you.

4. **YOUR STORY CORE RAISES YOUR VIBRATION.**

Because your life and story are mirrors of one another, the simple act of writing your Story Core will immediately begin to change the story you're carrying inside. The vibrations of your daily thoughts, feelings, and actions will rise, as will your receptivity to more positive experiences that match the vibration of your Story Core, simply by crafting it.

Instructions for Crafting Your Story Core

You have many different positive experiences that you could choose from, but following these instructions will ensure that you choose the *right* Story Core—the one that feels the *most* inspiring, uplifting, and supportive of the dreams in your ELS Intention.

1. WRITE YOUR LIST OF POSITIVE MEMORIES.

You'll begin by writing your List of Positive Memories, which includes the most positive experiences you can remember. The list can be as long as you want. Your List of Positive Memories will help you to choose your Story Core, and it will also provide you with an easy way to pull more positive experiences into your ELS in later stages—experiences that aren't in the forefront of your mind, simply because they're not yet playing a prominent role in your narrative.

2. FREEWRITE POTENTIAL STORY CORES.

After writing your List of Positive Memories, you'll circle two to three experiences that feel like potential Story Cores—those memories that light you up the most—and freewrite up to one page about each experience. Write whatever comes to mind without planning or thinking about it ahead of time, aiming to describe the lessons the experience taught you and the meaning inside of it. Also, try to write in a way that would make sense to your Ideal Reader—someone without any previous knowledge of you or context for understanding why the experience is significant. After completing your potential Story Core freewrites, you'll pick the one that feels best and most compatible with your ELS Intention.

3. **EXPRESS YOUR EMOTIONS FULLY.**

One thing you might experience when freewriting a potential Story Core is holding yourself back from fully expressing your emotions on the page. If this happens, your Ideal Reader won't understand how significant the experience was for you, which means you won't fully understand how significant the experience was for you, either. Make sure that your feelings are clear and compelling in each of your freewrites, as this will strengthen the power of your positive memories to protect you from darkness.

4. **CHOOSE YOUR STORY CORE.**

When deciding on your Story Core, make sure that it's compatible with and most supportive of the results in your ELS Intention. If one of the primary results in your ELS Intention is to manifest greater abundance in your life, you'll need a Story Core that describes a time when you felt abundant. If the main focus of your ELS Intention is to attract true love, you'll need a Story Core that describes a time when you felt truly loved. If the main result in your ELS Intention is to create a successful career as a dancer, you'll need a Story Core that describes a time when you felt amazing and comfortable in your own skin while dancing.

If you have difficulty choosing which experiences are best to freewrite about, talk through your List of Positive Memories with a trusted friend or writing partner and ask them for feedback about which memories light you up the most when you talk about them. You can also ask for the same kind of feedback in deciding which of your potential Story Core freewrites should become your actual Story Core.

Path Skipping in Chapter 6

One way to skip off the path in this chapter is by assuming that the *first* Story Core that comes to mind is "the one," and thus, avoid exploring any other options (by not writing your List of Positive Memories or your two to three potential Story Core freewrites). Sometimes the first Story Core that pops into your mind is best, but oftentimes, you won't know for sure which Story Core is best for you until completing all the steps of your ELS Written Exercise. My clients have often been surprised by the Story Core that ended up feeling right to them and you might be, too!

The most significant way to skip off the path in this stage of the process is to use a *negative* experience as your Story Core in an attempt to turn it into a positive. People are often quick to point out that no experience is *purely* positive or negative, and they're right—it's all a matter of perspective, which is what the ELS Method is all about.

However, choosing a Story Core that doesn't *automatically* and immediately make you feel good is a sneaky way to skip off the path. It's very hard to attract what you want—maybe even impossible—when you've got a negative experience dominating your story. As we've discussed, it *is* important to include "negative" experiences in your ELS that feel essential to represent, but it's equally important to *not* make those experiences your Story Core. The strongest story always wins, and in order for your dreams to come true, your story needs a center that effortlessly makes you feel victorious.

Chapter 6 ELS Written Exercise

Before you begin, create a sacred, comfortable space to work. Turn off your devices and make sure you won't be interrupted for at least an hour. Read your ELS Intention aloud, and update it, if needed. Then, complete the following:

1. Write your List of Positive Memories by hand, including as many as you can think of.

2. Circle the two to three memories on your List of Positive Memories that feel best and most supportive of your ELS Intention.

3. Freewrite, by hand, up to a page about each of your two to three potential Story Cores, describing the lesson each experience taught you and why it is so meaningful to you. Make sure you capture the emotional impact of the experience.

4. Choose your Story Core by asking yourself, *Which freewrite feels most inspiring, uplifting, and supportive of my ELS Intention?*

5. Type all of your responses for the questions above into your *ELS Written Exercises* document.

6. Have a trusted friend or writing partner provide you with feedback to ensure that you followed the instructions for this ELS Written Exercise.

7. Add any significant breakthroughs or results that you experience under the Breakthroughs and Results area of your *ELS Written Exercises* document.

in the bank	Visit www.TheELSResourceBank.com to download a printable version of the *Chapter 6 ELS Written Exercise*, which includes the instructions from this chapter that you'll need to complete your exercise.

Seven

Turning Your Greatest Current Challenge into a Magical New Reality

The happy ending of the fairy tale, the myth, and the divine comedy of the soul is to be read, not as a contradiction, but as a transcendence of the universal tragedy of man.

—JOSEPH CAMPBELL

In the movie *Dumbo*, a young elephant feels depressed and overburdened by the enormous size of his ears—ears that cause him to be ridiculed, isolated, and even separated from his own mother. Timothy Q. Mouse tries to cheer Dumbo up, by saying, "The very things that held you down are going to carry you up and up!" And by the end of Dumbo's story, the mouse turned out to be right: Dumbo's enormous ears became the very thing that allowed him to be admired by many, soar through the air, and reunite with his mother.

Similarly, whatever challenge you're currently facing—no matter how difficult, unchangeable, or inescapable it might seem—can become the very thing that lifts you up and allows you to fly. In your ELS

Written Exercise for this chapter, you'll identify your Greatest Current Challenge, answer a series of questions about it, and craft your Fairy Tale Freewrite. These questions, and the moral of your fairy tale, will transform your perspective and allow you to craft a New Reality Statement that resolves the inner conflict that lays beneath your challenge. This exercise helps you to transcend your challenge and live from the growth opportunity that it offers you.

Creating My New Reality

In the preface of this book, I talked about a journey I made to the Amazon rainforest shortly after college. What I didn't share in the preface is how the circumstances under which I had to *leave* the Amazon—and the way I viewed those circumstances—gave rise to the greatest, decade-long challenge of my life.

When I first heard about the Achuar tribe in college, I'd never felt more powerfully called toward anything in my life. The Achuar are a "dream culture," which means that they believe dreams are more real than waking life, because dreams are the most direct way for Spirit to speak to us. The Achuar also believe that every human needs a dream that they're working towards every day in waking life, in order to feel fulfilled.

Two years after first learning about the Achuar, I was offered a volunteer English teacher position in their territory. I sold everything I owned, jumped on a plane, and had the time of my life teaching English and then training to become a guide. For the first time in my life, I felt at peace every day. In every moment, I felt connected to a higher, loving consciousness that ran through everything. When I was offered a year-long contract to be a tour guide, leading journeys in Achuar territory, it felt like my Greatest Dream had come true.

But it all took a terrible turn when two weeks into my new position as a guide, I got stuck in quicksand and tore the ligaments in my knee while trying to pull free. My knee swelled to the size of a grapefruit, and I could barely walk—let alone guide tourists through the jungle. Heartbroken, I returned home to the States so I could get a "regular" job, with health insurance, and get knee surgery. I didn't know if or when I would ever return to the jungle.

It felt like I'd been kicked out of the Garden of Eden. I had finally gotten what I wanted, only to have it ripped away. At least, that was the story I told myself for a long time, without being fully aware of it. It was a story that carried the message, *I don't get to have what I want, and if I do, it'll just be taken away from me anyway.* The power of that story was that it prevented me from allowing myself to pursue anything that I truly wanted—including a return to the jungle one day. Because of the strength of my unconscious perspective, I didn't even feel comfortable reaching out to the people I knew and cared about in the Amazon. Perhaps worse, I didn't allow myself to recreate the feeling of peace and happiness *here* that I'd felt *there*. Why bother if it was just going to get ripped away again?

It wasn't until I began writing my ELS that I came to see how my perspective about leaving the jungle was holding me prisoner in a painful reality that left no space for my dreams. When I realized this, and decided to look for a new way of seeing the experience, my first thought was, *There's no way to put a positive spin on this story… there can't possibly be a silver lining.* But when I encouraged myself to try, the new perspective came to mind pretty quickly (as is almost always the case).

I realized that I probably wasn't the only person who had traveled to the Amazon and felt disoriented upon returning home. Maybe I was supposed to use my story to close the gap between who I knew myself to be in this culture and what I had discovered about myself in the Amazon. And maybe I was supposed to help other people do the same. Perhaps Source—and the jungle itself—really did have a plan for me that wasn't intended to make me suffer, but rather, was intended to help me soar. That simple yet profound shift in my perspective led to a magical new reality where I not only returned to the Amazon, but also wrote this book.

Why Finding Your Silver Lining is So Important

The idea of finding the "silver lining" in your Greatest Current Challenge can feel surface-level, new-agey, and even naive—like you're bypassing the problem rather than truly facing it. However, the ELS Written Exercise in this chapter will help you to move *through* your challenge, as opposed to bypassing it, by aligning with the meaning and opportunity inside of your Greatest Current Challenge, resolving the inner conflict behind it, and turning it into a magical new reality—all in a way that feels authentic and eye-opening, rather than dismissive and avoidant. This turn-around represents a paradigm shift that is crucial for success with the ELS Method, since your Greatest Current Challenge is also the greatest obstacle toward manifesting your Greatest Dreams.

The benefit of finding the meaning, gift, or growth opportunity inside your Greatest Current Challenge is that it allows you to accept the fact that you're facing it. And you *can't* overcome a challenge without first accepting it. Without acceptance, your challenge will feel random and meaningless, and you'll be a sitting duck for that same type of challenge to hit you again. You'll always be on the lookout for how and when that problem will repeat itself, and your negative anticipation will become a self-fulfilling prophecy. However, when you surrender to the fact that you're experiencing the challenge for a reason and you find the magical meaning inside of it, you'll stop attracting similar experiences because the reason for your challenge will have disappeared.

Resolving the inner conflict behind your Greatest Current Challenge is also crucial to overcoming it. Even challenges that you seemingly have no control over—like health problems or other people causing drama in your life—arise from inner conflict. For every challenge you face, there will be something truly positive that the challenge *allows* you to have, as well as something truly positive that the challenge *prevents* you from having. The key to resolving that inner conflict is to let all parts of you know that you can have *both* truly positive things—that currently feel incompatible—at the same time.

For example, if you're an actor who's not booking the lead roles that you want, that challenge is *allowing* you to have plenty of time at home with your loved ones. But at the same time, it's *preventing* you from doing the work you love in a meaningful way. It's because these two truly positive things—time with your loved ones and the work you love—feel mutually exclusive that you experience inner conflict. But when you come to understand that your seemingly incompatible desires can not only be fulfilled simultaneously, but that they're *meant* to be fulfilled simultaneously, the inner conflict can dissolve, and so can the challenge. In the ELS Written Exercise for this chapter, you will expose the internal conflict inside of your Greatest Current Challenge and craft a New Reality Statement that paves the way toward inner peace, allowing you to have *all of the things* that are truly positive and important to you.

It's okay if you don't immediately and completely see your challenge as a great gift from Source. It's okay if you grumble a little or feel resistant to completing your ELS Written Exercise. You *can* regret that you have to experience a challenge, while at the same time see the opportunity that it offers you. That said, after completing your ELS Written Exercise for this chapter, it won't be long before your resistance to seeing the opportunity inside of your challenge melts, and you arrive at a place of gratitude for having experienced it; that's when you'll know that you've truly moved beyond it.

Instructions for Crafting Your New Reality Statement

In your ELS Written Exercise for this chapter, you'll answer a series of questions about the greatest challenge that you're currently facing, and your answers will be used to fill in a template for crafting your New Reality Statement.

1. **NAME THE GREATEST CURRENT CHALLENGE YOU'RE FACING.**

   Your Greatest Current Challenge can be in any area of your life, including your love life, career, family, finances, physical health, creativity, spirituality, and emotional well-being. You may be facing a number of challenges, but be sure to choose the *one* problem that feels *most pressing right now*—the one that keeps you up at night and drains your precious energy. This challenge *can* be something that originated in the past, as long as it's still weighing on you in the present. For example, your Greatest Current Challenge could be residual trauma from a divorce *in the past* that's causing you to close your heart to new love *in the present.* When describing the problem, be sure to use negative language, such as, *I can't open my heart to love* or *I'll never get over my heartbreak.*

2. **IDENTIFY THE ROOT EXPERIENCE.**

   Next, you'll answer two questions: Why do you imagine you have this problem? And what Root Experience is underlying it? The purpose of these questions is *not* to judge or blame yourself for having the problem, but rather to explore, with curiosity, what past experiences might have given rise to the problem. When you identify the root of your problem, in the context of your larger story, your problem will no longer look random and inexplicable, and you will no longer feel so powerless to change it. You'll be able to see that you are the common denominator in all of your experiences, and so you *do* have the power to overcome your challenge.

3. **NAME WHAT YOU WANT INSTEAD OF THE PROBLEM.**

   After exploring the Root Experience that underlies your Greatest Current Challenge, you'll name what you want *instead* of the problem. This part is usually pretty easy, just be sure to use *positive* language when describing what you want (rather than negative language about what you *don't* want), as in, *I want to feel confident and optimistic about starting my own business.*

4. **RESOLVE THE INNER CONFLICT.**

Next, you'll answer a series of questions that help you to identify and resolve the inner conflict behind your challenge. One of those questions is: what might happen that is *negative* if you get what you want instead of this problem? While that question may sound crazy at first, when you sit with it, an important answer will always come to you. One of my clients, Julie, had been dealing with a health challenge that made her walking increasingly difficult (sometimes impossible) over the past several years. When we started working together, her number one goal was to be able to walk easily again. When I asked Julie what might happen that is *negative* if she could walk easily again, it took her a minute to even consider the possibility that anything bad could come out of being able to walk easily. But after giving it some thought, she realized that people were *so* nice, compassionate, and helpful to her now (because she had so much trouble walking) and she didn't want that to go away! So the negative expectation Julie was carrying was that if she was healed, people wouldn't be nice to her anymore. However, once she crafted her New Reality Statement, she was no longer afraid of that possibility—she realized she could walk easily *and* people would still be nice to her.

5. **IDENTIFY THE GIFT OR GROWTH OPPORTUNITY INSIDE OF THE PROBLEM.**

The last question you'll answer is: What gift or growth opportunity does this problem offer you? If you feel terrified of starting a new business, for example, your growth opportunity might be to take a courageous leap of faith. If you're going through a breakup, your growth opportunity might be to learn how to love yourself even *more* than you love you love your romantic partner. If you were just betrayed, and ignored the red flags you saw early on, your growth opportunity might be to honor and listen to your intuition, without fail. No matter what challenge you're facing, it always offers you the gift of a growth opportunity.

6. **CRAFT YOUR FAIRY TALE FREEWRITE AND DISTILL ITS WISDOM.**

Your Fairy Tale Freewrite will allow your deep inner knowing to provide you with a solution to your Greatest Current Challenge, an energetic blueprint for moving beyond it, through the use of metaphor. It's very important to freewrite this story without thinking about what you'll write ahead of time. It's also important to begin your Fairy Tale Freewrite with, *Once upon a time, there was a girl/boy/angel…*, and then write a story about how the main character (a fantasy version of yourself) magically overcomes their Greatest Current Challenge. Anything is possible in your fairy tale: there might be angels, dragons, unicorns, fairies, an evil queen, or a monster man, and you may have special powers. After writing your Fairy Tale Freewrite, you'll distill the moral of the story into one sentence, which will ensure that your Fairy Tale Freewrite eclipses whatever powerful negative story you're currently telling yourself that has kept you stuck in your challenge. You'll realize, because it came out so easily in this magical little story, that the solution to your problem was inside of you all along.

7. **FILL IN THE TEMPLATE FOR CREATING YOUR NEW REALITY STATEMENT.**

Finally, you'll craft your New Reality Statement by filling in a template, using your answers from the previous series of questions.

After taking these steps, you'll find that your Greatest Current Challenge truly does hold a great opportunity inside of it, and that it's prompting you to transform your life in exactly those ways that are necessary to manifest your Greatest Dreams.

in the bank　Visit www.TheELSResourceBank.com to download *A Fairy Tale Freewrite Example* that illustrates the energy, tone, and language that will allow magic and wisdom to flow through your pen.

Path Skipping in Chapter 7

You might feel a lot of resistance to completing the ELS Written Exercise for this chapter, and find yourself thinking, *There is nothing even remotely positive that can come out of the greatest challenge I'm currently facing!* If that happens, pause and ask yourself, *Could there possibly be a silver lining?*

You might resist finding the gift inside of your challenge for fear that doing so is the equivalent of appreciating your challenge and thus, asking Source for more. However, using your challenge as a growth opportunity will *not* invite more of the same challenges. On the contrary, finding the gift inside of your challenge will lower your resistance to manifesting what you want *instead* of that challenge—you've already been incredibly clear with Source in your ELS Intention about what you want, and Source has heard you loud and clear.

Chapter 7 ELS Written Exercise

Before you begin, create a sacred, comfortable space to work. Turn off your devices and make sure you won't be interrupted for at least an hour. Read your ELS Intention aloud, and update it, if needed. Then, complete the following:

1. Name your Greatest Current Challenge, using negative language.

2. Identify the Root Experience behind your Greatest Current Challenge by answering these two questions: Why do you imagine you have this problem? And what Root Experience is underlying it?

3. What do you want instead of this problem? Be sure to use positive language.

4. What might happen that is *negative* if you get what you want instead of this problem?

5. What might happen that is *positive* if you get what you want instead of this problem?

6. What truly positive thing does this problem *allow* you to have?

7. What truly positive thing does this problem *prevent* you from having?

8. What gift or growth opportunity does this problem offer you?

9. Craft your Fairy Tale Freewrite by hand, where the main character (a fantasy version of yourself) overcomes their Greatest Current Challenge (which represents your own).

10. Distill the main lesson or wisdom from your Fairy Tale Freewrite into one sentence.

11. Create a New Reality Statement, by filling in the following template with your answers from above:

    Lately, I've been facing the challenge of _____ (insert answer from #1/the challenge). And I can see that _____ (insert answer from #2/the root of the challenge). And I can also see from where I am now that the gift in this challenge is _____ (insert answer from #8/the growth opportunity) and that the opportunity before me is to both have _____ (insert answer from #6/what the challenge allows you to have) AND _____ (insert answer from #7/what the problem prevents you from having) where _____ (insert answer from #5/what might happen that is positive). And I understand that _____ (insert your response to #10/the moral of your Fairy Tale Freewrite).

12. Afterwards, type your responses into your *ELS Written Exercises* document.

13. Have a trusted friend or writing partner provide you with feedback to ensure that you followed the instructions for this ELS Written Exercise.

14. Add any significant breakthroughs or results that you experience under the Breakthroughs and Results area of your *ELS Written Exercises* document.

---

in the bank

Visit www.TheELSResourceBank.com to download a printable version of the *Chapter 7 ELS Written Exercise,* which includes the instructions from this chapter that you'll need to complete your exercise.

Eight
Discovering Your Greatest Dreams

The greater danger for most of us is not that our aim is too high and we miss it, but that it is too low and we reach it.

—MICHELANGELO

In order to write yourself into your dreams, you first have to identify—with certainty—what your Greatest Dreams *are*. It's often said that the journey of life is more important than the destination. And while that may be true, your destination still *matters*. For your journey to be truly fulfilling, you have to be traveling toward dreams that are meaningful and aligned with your purpose; you have to be traveling toward your *Greatest* Dreams.

In the ELS Written Exercise for this chapter, you will complete four primary tasks. First, you'll create your Big Dreams List, which will get you in touch with *all* of your dreams. Then, you'll write your Best Possible Eulogy, which will separate those dreams that are *most* important to you from all the rest. After writing your Best Possible Eulogy, you will be able to easily choose the top three dreams, from your Big Dreams List, that represent your Greatest Dreams. Finally, you'll create your

Already Realized Dreams List, to strengthen your faith that your Greatest Dreams will come true, just as your previous dreams did.

People often tell me that after completing their ELS Written Exercise for this chapter, they suddenly started prioritizing their dreams, experiencing immediate traction, and in some cases, magically manifested one of their Greatest Dreams without any effort at all. This spontaneous momentum happens in large part because the act of writing about your dreams is a manifestation in and of itself—moving your dreams from the airy realm of thought to the physical reality of paper.

Debunking 4 of the Most Common Fears About Your Dreams

Your dreams, or heart's desires, are those that quietly and persistently call to you, whether you're in active pursuit of them or not. When you find yourself hiding, ignoring, or doubting your dreams, when you hold yourself back from going all-in, it's because deep down you're afraid of something bad that you imagine will happen if your dream *does* come true. The following list of dream-related fears are usually operating on an unconscious level, but reading about them will bring any that affect you to the light of your conscious awareness where the hold they have over you can begin to soften.

1. "I WILL DIE."

   There's an episode of *Seinfeld*, called "The Pilot" (part 2 of the 2-part episode finale of the fourth season) that addresses this common fear. In it, right after George and Jerry sell their TV pilot and begin filming, George notices something white on his lip and suddenly becomes convinced that he's going to die. He says to Jerry, "I told you that God would never let me be successful. I never should've written that pilot. Now the show will be a big hit, we'll make millions of dollars, and I'll be dead. Dead Jerry. Because of this."

This fear of dying immediately after achieving a great dream has surfaced with my clients more times than I can count. While this fear may sound absurd, it's actually reasonable: realizing your dreams elevates your life to a higher level, which actually *does* represent a death, of sorts. Realizing your dreams involves a dying-off of old ways of thinking, feeling, and behaving that simply can't come with you to a higher level.

Parts of you that over-identify with these "old ways" will anticipate this metaphorical death as a literal one, of your whole being. This anticipation can manifest as a fear of receiving a terminal diagnosis—as George feared—or getting hit by a bus or being eaten by a wild animal. The particulars don't matter as much as the rationale they lead to: you must avoid your dreams to stay alive. But the truth is, the process of realizing your dreams will give birth to lighter, freer, and more empowered ways of being that allow you to not only survive, but *thrive*.

2. **"THE POINT OF MY LIFE WILL BE OVER."**

You may also avoid pursuing your dreams for fear that if you realize them, you will no longer have a reason to exist, since your primary reason for incarnation will have been satisfied. However, this fear is rooted in a cultural lack of knowledge about the process of dream-fulfillment.

As we discussed in chapter 7, the Achuar people in the Amazon are a "dream culture," and thus, experts in the dream-fulfillment process. A central part of the Achuar culture is that every member of the tribe communes with the rainforest when they come of age to be given, or assigned, the dream they're meant to pursue. Then, they work toward that dream every day until it's fulfilled. Once the first dream is fulfilled, they commune with the forest *again* to receive their next dream. The Achuar understand a universal truth about dream fulfillment: it is a continuous cycle in which the fulfillment of one dream leads directly to the birth of another. And so, the point of your life is continually being renewed.

3. **"IF I FAIL, I'LL LOSE THE DREAM."**

    You might also fear, deep down, that if you truly give a dream your all, and fail, you won't even get to have the dream anymore. The idea of losing the dream completely is terrifying, because without a dream, you're faced with the painful possibility that you don't have a purpose after all.

    However, any heart-centered dream that you have is a sacred assignment from Source, and is thus meant to be pursued. *If* the pursuit of your dream doesn't work out in the way you'd originally hoped, the pursuit itself will have served a very important purpose: it will have led you to *another* dream that's even more important— a dream that you wouldn't have even been able to discover if not for the pursuit of the previous one. So, you never have to worry about being left without a dream that inspires you—Source will make sure that you always have one.

4. **"I WON'T LIKE MYSELF ANYMORE."**

    Another reason you might avoid a dream is for fear that it will bring you wealth and success, and in the process, turn you into a version of yourself that you don't like—someone who is selfish, greedy, and egotistical. For example, one of my clients, Ted, felt blocked around his dream of producing his own films, because he was afraid of becoming a "rich asshole" like his uncle. As a kid, Ted had promised himself *never* to be like his uncle, which meant never becoming rich. Once he became conscious of this fear, he was able to let the kid inside of himself know that there are many ways to be rich, and that he could be the kind of wealthy artist who was also kind, humble, and generous. So, if you realize that you're afraid of "losing yourself" when you realize a dream, know that realizing your dream is a journey, and that all journeys give you the opportunity to know yourself better and become even *more* of who you really are.

in the bank

Visit www.TheELSResourceBank.com to download *Additional Reasons You Might Fear Your Dreams.*

The Ideal Attitude Toward Your Dreams

In chapter 1, we talked about how relating to your dreams with a lot of attachment is what causes suffering—not the dreams themselves. It's worth reviewing and expanding upon this point again in this chapter, since it's been awhile.

When I was a kid, I watched *Tiny Toons*, and there was a character named Elmira whose sole desire in life was to hug, kiss, and smother cute, furry animals until their eyes were bulging out of their heads. As you might imagine (or remember), animals ran from her like hell fire. Similarly, your dreams will run from you if you relate to them with desperation. You'll know you're in a place of desperation with your dreams when you catch yourself thinking thoughts like, *This has to happen right now! I'm READY!! Why isn't my partner/money/success here yet?!* This attitude leaves you working against yourself rather than being in a place of receptivity. Eventually, you'll become disheartened, burned out, and give up—taking your failure as a sign that your dreams aren't meant to be.

On the other hand, your dreams will run eagerly toward you when you relate to them with an ideal attitude that's characterized by patience and optimism. With this attitude, you will always be looking for evidence that your dreams are on their way to you, and you'll surrender to *however* Source chooses to deliver. You'll know you're in a place of patience and optimism with your dreams, which makes you a magnet for them, when you notice yourself thinking thoughts like, *I know that this partner/money/success is happening for me. And I'm so excited to see how it all unfolds! It's going to be better than I could ever imagine.*

Your Big Dreams List

Your Big Dreams List includes everything that you would love to be, do, or have before you die. Your dreams can be in any area of your life—relationships, career, finances, creativity, and even states of being—and they can be anything at all, as long as they come from your heart. You can include as many dreams as you want on your Big Dreams List, so don't hold back. You might dream of becoming a dancer, finding true love, directing your first film, playing the harp, building an animal sanctuary, or opening a bakery that serves 101 different kinds of croissants (just be sure to call me if you make that last one happen!).

When creating your Big Dreams List, it's important to shoot for the moon, because when you want to change your reality, you can't afford to be "realistic." Now is the time to empower the soft, quiet voices inside of you that are often overpowered by rational thought, other people's doubts, and a million modern-day distractions. This list is your chance to give voice to each and every dream you've ever had—even the ones you've never admitted to anyone.

Be sure to write each of your dreams using positive language, as you did when writing your ELS Intention. If any of your dreams come out in negative language, convert them into positive language. For example, if you write, *My dream is to never be in a bad relationship again,* turn it into, *My dream is to have a healthy, loving relationship with a true partner.*

In chapter 1, we talked about the important difference between surface desires and heart's desires, but you don't have to worry about distinguishing between the two when writing your Big Dreams List—just write everything that comes to mind. If one of the dreams on your Big Dreams List *doesn't* actually come from your heart, that will soon become clear, and that surface desire will naturally fall away.

Your Best Possible Eulogy

Next, you'll write your Best Possible Eulogy, which will help you to get clear about which of the dreams on your Big Dreams List are *most* important to you. The words "Best Possible Eulogy" can sound scary, because we avoid talking about death in our culture, but this exercise will allow you to reflect on your life, from the perspective of your soul, to answer the question, *What is truly most important to me, as a spiritual being?*

What originally inspired me to create this exercise was a story I heard about Alfred Nobel, who made his fortune by inventing dynamite and becoming the world's largest weapons manufacturer. In 1888, Alfred's brother Ludvig died, and the following day, a French newspaper erroneously reported *Alfred* as having died, rather than his brother. The headline famously announced, "THE MERCHANT OF DEATH IS DEAD." The combined tragedy of losing his brother and glimpsing how horribly history would have remembered him if he *had* died that day inspired Alfred to make massive changes in his life moving forward. Eight years later, Alfred Nobel signed his last will and testament, leaving 94% of his assets to establish the five Nobel Prizes.

Your Best Possible Eulogy allows you to get similarly clear about what you want your legacy to be, without having to experience the trauma Alfred Nobel did. Before you begin, you'll imagine that you've passed away peacefully and are witnessing your ideal funeral, memorial, or celebration of life in spirit. You'll imagine that all of the dreams on your Big Dreams List came true before you died, and that now, someone very dear to you is delivering your eulogy. You'll write a couple of paragraphs from your loved one's perspective (in first person) about the profound impact you had on their life, making sure to include the specific things you did and said that moved and inspired them. These details will make your Best Possible Eulogy feel grounded and real, and it will naturally and effortlessly highlight your Greatest Dreams.

It's important to understand that a eulogy is not the same thing as an obituary. Obituaries are written in third person and usually lack emotion. Obituaries state basic facts and provide a sense of finality and respect, but they're not particularly moving. They don't get to the heart of who a person was, or describe how they touched those who loved them. A eulogy, on the other hand, is a firsthand, heartfelt expression of a loved one's life and influence, often delivered through tears, by someone who deeply loved the departed.

In case you're concerned, writing your Best Possible Eulogy will *not* bring about your untimely death by virtue of the Law of Attraction, because that is not the *intention* of this exercise. The intention of writing your Best Possible Eulogy is to help you live a long and happy life, where you fulfill your Greatest Dreams, and Source knows that.

in the bank

Visit www.TheELSResourceBank.com to download an *Example of a Big Dreams List and Best Possible Eulogy.*

Your Greatest Dreams

After writing your Best Possible Eulogy, you'll read your Big Dreams List again and choose the dreams that now feel most important—those are your Greatest Dreams. While you can write as many dreams as you want on your *Big* Dreams List, it's essential to limit yourself to choosing only a few *Greatest* Dreams. This limitation is important: one of the most insidious forms of self-sabotage is pursuing too many dreams at the same time, which prevents you from making significant progress on any one of them.

You'll notice that many of the dreams on your Big Dreams List aren't mentioned in your Best Possible Eulogy. Conversely, you may have dreams that show up in your Best Possible Eulogy that weren't mentioned in your Big Dreams List. Either way, certain dreams will stand out as being more important to you than you previously realized. This new awareness will cause a major shift in how you prioritize your time, focus, and attention every day.

Also, while it may sound obvious, make sure that you choose only Greatest Dreams that you are *not* already experiencing (or experiencing to the degree that you would like). For example, if you write, *making a difference in the world*, but you're already a life coach and make a difference every day in the lives of your clients, you'd need to choose a more specific dream. You'd need to choose a dream that involves making a difference in a way that you *haven't* yet accomplished, such as, *being a motivational speaker* or *writing a book*. And if a dream that shows up in your Best Possible Eulogy feels many years away, it's important to still include it on your Greatest Dreams list, so that you can build the story that brings it to life at the perfect time.

Your Already Realized Dreams List

Your next task is to make a list of every dream you've had in the past that has *already* come true. It's amazing how often Already Realized Dreams fail to be a focal point in my clients' 5-Page Freewrites —people tend to overlook the fact that the life they're living now is, in many ways, the life they used to dream of! Your Already Realized Dreams List will be incorporated into your ELS in later stages to remind you of what a powerful creator you are, by reminding you of all the things you used to dream of that have already come true. Appreciating what you've already manifested—in writing—will make you much more hopeful, optimistic, and receptive to your Greatest Dreams, as well as confident in your ability to make them come true.

Deciphering Between Your Greatest Dreams and the Dreams in Your ELS Intention

After completing your ELS Written Exercise for this chapter, it's important to update your ELS Intention. You'll either want to change the dreams that are inside of it, or change the way you describe them. Also, there's an important distinction between your Greatest Dreams and the dreams in your ELS Intention: your Greatest Dreams should be those that you want to manifest before you die (but may be several years down the line), whereas the dreams in your ELS Intention should be those you want to manifest *right now*. For example, if one of your Greatest Dreams is to create a retreat center, but you've not yet led your first retreat, *leading a retreat* should be one of the dreams in your ELS Intention, while *opening a retreat center* should be one of your Greatest Dreams.

Path Skipping in Chapter 8

The primary reason you may feel resistance in this stage of the process is due to an unconscious fear that there's a limited amount of love, success, and happiness available in the world. You may think that taking more than "your share" of the pie will leave too little for everyone else, but that's not how it works. As we talked about in chapter 1, love, happiness, and success are *not* limited resources. Realizing your dreams won't take anything away from anyone else; on the contrary, it will inspire others to achieve their dreams, as well.

Chapter 8 ELS Written Exercise

Before you begin, create a sacred, comfortable space to work. Turn off your devices and make sure you won't be interrupted for at least an hour. Read your ELS Intention aloud, and update it, if needed. Then, complete the following:

1. Write your Big Dreams List by hand.

2. Describe the setting of your ideal funeral, memorial, or celebration of life and name the person you'd like to see deliver your eulogy.

3. Write your Best Possible Eulogy by hand.

4. Identify your Greatest Dreams (those few that feel most important to you now, after having written your Best Possible Eulogy).

5. Write your Already Realized Dreams List.

6. Type your responses to each of the above into your *ELS Written Exercises* document.

7. Have a trusted friend or writing partner provide you with feedback to ensure that you followed the instructions for this ELS Written Exercise.

8. Add any new breakthroughs or results that you experience under the Breakthroughs and Results area of your *ELS Written Exercises* document, beginning each entry with the date.

in the bank

Visit www.TheELSResourceBank.com to download a printable version of the *Chapter 8 ELS Written Exercise*, which includes the instructions from this chapter that you'll need to complete your exercise.

Nine

Assembling Your ELS

With a pencil and paper, I could revise the world.

—ALISON LURIE

In Japan, there's an art form called Kintsugi, or "golden repair," in which broken pieces of pottery are put back together again using lacquer and precious metals. When you look at a piece of Kintsugi art, you can see how it's *more* beautiful, rather than less, for having once been broken.

This step of the ELS Method is like the first step of creating a piece of Kintsugi art, where you begin to put the "broken pieces" of your story back together again—a story you have been breaking down and recreating since you began using the ELS Method. As you assemble your ELS, using the Copy-and-Paste ELS Template, you'll begin to feel the life-changing beauty, power, and potential of what your story will soon become.

The Pull Between Two Stories

Your story will be in a major state of flux by this stage of the process, not only on paper, but also inside of you. Since you began using the ELS Method, you've been breaking down your old story, but because your new story is not yet fully formed, you'll have *two* stories right now, rather than one, and you'll feel yourself pulled between them. You'll have one foot in a world where your old story dominates and the other foot in a world where your new story is starting to reign, and your mind will reflect that duality.

Sometimes, you'll notice your mind, out of habit, attempting to run the same old mental tapes, full of negative thoughts that align with your old story. But then, you'll notice that those thoughts don't stick—they won't feel as convincing as they used to. You'll wonder, *Wait a minute... what is my story?* At the same time, you'll notice your mind starting to run *new* tapes filled with positive thoughts that align with your new story (that is starting to take form)—thoughts you've never had before. It's important to understand that this mental back-and-forth is completely normal in this stage of the process; it's an indication that you're moving from one story to another, which is wonderful, and you will soon feel the magic of having *one* powerful story that fully aligns your mind with the manifestation of your Greatest Dreams.

Instructions for Using the Copy-and-Paste ELS Template

The process of assembling the first draft of your ELS is a little awkward; it will feel messy and disjointed and—at the same time—exciting and full of potential. As you follow the instructions below, you can expect to experience additional breakthroughs and big shifts in your perspective.

1. SET UP THE BASICS.

Create a document titled *My ELS*, and include today's date in the title. Open the document, and at the top of the page, write "My Commitment Statement," and copy your most current Commitment Statement underneath (from your chapter 1 ELS Written Exercise). Then, skip a line and write "My ELS Intention," and copy your most current ELS Intention underneath. Skip another line and write "Completed ELS Letters," followed by each of the names of the people with whom you have completed ELS Letters. On the next line, write "ELS Letters Yet to Complete," followed by the names of people you *haven't* yet completed ELS Letters with (from your ELS Letters List in your chapter 5 ELS Written Exercise). On the next line, write the header "Message List" and leave the space underneath blank for now (your messages will be added under this header in the next chapter).

2. **ADD YOUR 5-PAGE FREEWRITE AND STORY CORE.**

Below the space under "Message List," write the heading "My ELS" and then copy and paste your entire 5-Page Freewrite from chapter 3 underneath. If you're working with a writing partner and they made comments on your story (about confusing areas that need clarification, for example), make sure to include those comments in your *My ELS* document, so you can address them. Next, go back to your Chapter 6 ELS Written Exercise and copy all of the content from your Story Core freewrite *into* your 5-Page Freewrite, where it happened chronologically. For example, if your Story Core experience happened when you were twenty years old, paste it into the part of your story where you were around that age. When your see your Story Core *inside* of your 5-Page Freewrite, the contrast between the "dark" and "light" elements of your story will become more apparent, and you'll likely experience additional breakthroughs.

3. **ADD ESSENTIAL STATEMENTS ABOUT YOUR PARENTS.**

Revisit your Chapter 4 ELS Written Exercise and copy and paste each of your Parent Freewrites into the beginning of your 5-Page Freewrite. The first few sentences of your ELS need to be about *you*, not your parents. So, place your Parent Freewrites *after* where you talk about being born and *before* where you discuss your childhood. Then, distill your Parent Freewrites down to a couple of sentences each, including only what feels most important about your parents—information that will help your Ideal Reader understand how your parents' backstories have influenced your own.

4. **ADD THE ROOT EXPERIENCE BEHIND YOUR GREATEST CURRENT CHALLENGE.**

Look at your response to #2 from your chapter 7 ELS Written Exercise, in which you describe the Root Experience that is underlying your Greatest Current Challenge. If that experience is *not* already described in your 5-Page Freewrite, describe it now in a couple of sentences, wherever it happened chronologically in the story.

5. **ADD YOUR ALREADY REALIZED DREAMS.**

Look at your response to #5 from your chapter 8 ELS Written Exercise, in which you list your dreams that have already come true. For each of your Already Realized Dreams, insert a sentence into your 5-Page Freewrite about the first time you remember having that dream (before it came true). Then, insert a sentence into your 5-Page Freewrite describing how and when that dream manifested (wherever it happened chronologically). For example, if one of your Already Realized Dreams is having been in a movie, you can write a sentence about having had that dream in elementary school, in the early childhood part of your story. Then, you can describe the experience of watching yourself on the big screen later, whenever *that* happened chronologically. Make sure that you include a sentence in the story about when you first had the dream *and* a sentence about when it came true for each dream on your Already Realized Dreams List.

6. **RELOCATE YOUR BREAKTHROUGHS AND RESULTS.**

Go to your *ELS Written Exercises* document and cut the "Breakthroughs and Results" header and all of the content in that section—which you've been collecting throughout the process—and paste it at the bottom of your *My ELS* document. From now on, you'll record additional breakthroughs and results here, starting each entry with the date it occurred. If you notice any breakthroughs or results missing from your list, add them now.

7. **MAKE A HOME FOR ORBS.**

I borrowed the term "orbs" from Diana Gabaldon, author of the *Outlander* novels, who uses this word to describe pieces of a story that come to mind as she's writing, that don't have a home yet. After your "Breakthroughs and Results" section, you'll write the header "Orbs," and follow it with bulleted notes about pieces of your story that come to mind as you edit—that aren't currently in your ELS—such as, *Camp-out with Dad when he taught me to make a fire.* These memories will be "parked" in the Orbs area in case you want to integrate them into your ELS later.

8. **CREATE YOUR *ELS OVERFLOW* DOCUMENT.**

Lastly, create a document titled *ELS Overflow,* which is where you'll place content that is more appropriate for a longer version of your story, such as a memoir. As you're working on your ELS, there will be times when you feel inspired to write *more* about a memory or time period in your life than is appropriate for your ELS. For example, if you feel inspired to write a few paragraphs about the first play you were in, you can keep a few sentences about that experience in your ELS and move the rest to *ELS Overflow.*

Instructions for Basic Edits to Your ELS

Moving forward, I won't talk about your 5-Page Freewrite (which will always exist in its original form in your *ELS Written Exercises* document), because the version you're working on now has already evolved into the first draft of your ELS! After assembling your ELS, you'll spend a couple hours editing it in *only* the specific ways described below. You *won't* be fine-tuning or wordsmithing. That kind of editing is a waste of time at this stage of the process, because you won't yet have identified the messages that will dictate what stays in your completed ELS and what gets cut (that will happen in the next chapter).

1. KEEP YOUR ELS TIDY.

It's amazing how often I have to (gently) encourage my clients to tidy up their *My ELS* documents... I once even had to ask a client for example, to stop writing in all caps, because it was challenging for me to provide helpful feedback when it felt like I was being screamed at! A messy ELS filled with editing no-no's is an excellent way to prevent yourself from experiencing the breakthroughs that inherently come at this stage of the process. So in addition to *not* writing in all caps, keep your ELS neat by making sure that all the text is in the same font and size, that spelling and punctuation errors are kept to a minimum, and that random notes in the story are moved to Orbs or your *ELS Overflow*.

2. MAKE SURE YOUR ELS IS IN CHRONOLOGICAL ORDER.

It's important that your entire ELS be in chronological order, because jumping around in time will prevent breakthroughs, and it will also interfere with your ability to use the editing techniques (in future stages) that I designed to help you believe in your dreams. For example, if you have a paragraph in your ELS about all of your experiences that involve riding horses (from early childhood through high school) and another paragraph about what school was like (from early childhood through high school), much of the content in both paragraphs will be out of chronological order. While it may seem like a good idea to arrange your story by topic, re-arranging these subjects according to chronological order will help you to integrate your life experiences more fully and bring new awareness to important connections in your story that you couldn't see before.

3. **MAKE SURE THAT REALIZATIONS ARE IN THE RIGHT PLACE.**

Make sure that all realizations in your story are in the correct place chronologically, according to *when they happened*. It's incredibly common to immediately follow a description of a childhood experience with a realization that you had about that experience, as an adult. For example, let's say you have this passage in your ELS: *My sister and I were physically and psychologically abused by our father throughout our entire childhoods. That's probably why I became such a great therapist. After graduating high school, I moved as far away from home as I could.* The realization about why you're a good therapist would need to be moved to a later time in your ELS, when you had that realization. If you experienced that realization *after* starting the ELS Method, you would move it to the Breakthroughs and Results section of your ELS so that it could be properly integrated into your story later. One important reason for this rule, of keeping realizations in chronological order, is that it helps the younger aspects of you to feel honored and validated. Realizations about the meaning of a past challenge, at the time you're first describing the challenge, can make the younger parts of you that are still experiencing that challenge beyond time feel as though their experience is being dismissed, diminished, and devalued.

4. **GET FEEDBACK ON YOUR ELS TO CLARIFY CONFUSION.**

It's very important to receive feedback in this stage of the process, because it's so much easier for someone else to see the parts of your story that are unclear than it is for you to see them. For example, say you wrote, *I had a recurring nightmare for 10 years,* in your ELS without mentioning what the nightmare was about. In this case, *you* would know what the nightmare was about, but your Ideal Reader wouldn't have a clue, so they wouldn't understand the significance of the nightmare in your story. When you clarify each part of your ELS that is unclear to your Ideal Reader, your story will become even more clear to *you.*

5. FILL THE HOLES IN YOUR ELS.

When you read over your newly-assembled ELS, you'll notice obvious gaps, especially before and after content that was moved into your 5-Page Freewrite from other places. In some cases the inserted content will flow nicely with what's around it, but other times, it will need a transition statement before or after it. For example, you may jump from talking about getting married to talking about getting divorced, without mentioning why your marriage ended. Without any explanation, your Ideal Reader might wonder whether there was abuse, or cheating. You wouldn't have to add an entire page about all of your marital problems to fill that hole; a sentence or two about the primary issue that led to your separation would suffice, such as, *We had happy moments here and there, but she was never affectionate with me, and I felt unwanted.* Or you may notice a larger hole in your story, where you skipped an entire decade, perhaps because you feel like it was a wasted one. You could fill a hole like that with a single sentence: *There was a lot of sex, drugs, and rock and roll for the next ten years.* It's okay if these transitions are rough and ineloquent—they just need to be there. Also, you may notice that the ending of your story feels like a "hole" in and of itself right now, because it ends randomly; that's normal and it will be addressed in chapter 12 when you craft your Ideal Ending.

Reverse Patterns that Manifest in Writing

In chapter 3, we talked about how fascinating it is that patterns in your life will manifest through the *way you write* your story, and how it's equally fascinating to watch those patterns shift in your life by simply altering them on the page. I shared Sean's story about how he shifted the pattern of feeling like an outsider in his life by changing that pattern in the way he wrote his ELS. Now, you'll do the same, by spending some time reversing any negative patterns you notice in writing.

The most common pattern that manifests in writing—which everyone experiences to one degree or another—is disorganization. Your story, and thus life, will become more organized simply by following the editing instructions that we've already covered. Every client I've coached through the ELS Method has experienced this shift, where they suddenly can't stop themselves from cleaning out their closets, sorting through old paperwork, and taking loads of donations to the thrift store. This natural impulse to organize your life is a direct result of having a more organized story.

Another common pattern that manifests in writing is trying to impress people. If you notice yourself making an effort to sound witty or poetic in your ELS, you will likely see a similar pattern in your life of "trying too hard," because you don't feel interesting or "good enough." In Barbara Ueland's book, *On Writing Well*, she suggests writing how you would speak to 7th graders at a campout. You wouldn't try to impress them with big words, you'd speak plainly and simply. When you take this advice, and simplify the areas of your story where you notice a pattern of trying to impress people, you'll start to feel like you're more than enough in your daily life, just as you are.

You could also have a pattern of feeling unsafe that manifests in writing. When I first read my client Rachel's ELS, I noticed a pattern where she immediately followed positive experiences with traumatic ones, which always made me feel as if a bomb had gone off in the middle of the sentence. As a reader, I felt unable to relax. I was traveling through her story on high-alert, which was exactly how Rachel felt as she moved through life: she expected something bad to happen just when things were starting to get good (and it often did). Rachel transformed this pattern by describing the traumas she endured in clear and simple ways, separate from her positive experiences, using transition statements that acted as cushions. These "boundaries" that she incorporated into her written story had the effect of making her feel safer and more at peace in her daily life.

If you have a pattern of making yourself small in life, you'll do the same thing in your story: sell yourself short, downplay your accomplishments, and leave many of them out altogether. When you transform this pattern in writing, by appreciating yourself and adding or highlighting your accomplishments, you'll naturally begin to live your life in a "bigger", more empowered way. You'll begin to let yourself shine.

To reverse any old pattern in writing, simply ask yourself what the *opposite* of that pattern is and change your writing to reflect the new pattern. Like magic, that old pattern will begin to transform in your daily life, as well.

Path Skipping in Chapter 9

The most common form of Path Skipping in this stage is not allowing yourself to move on to chapter 10, because your ELS isn't perfect yet. However, it's not even possible for your ELS to become perfect in this stage, since as I mentioned earlier, you won't yet know what will make the cut in your final ELS (that happens in the next chapter).

Another way you might skip off the path in this stage is by receiving feedback from someone without telling them—specifically—what kind of feedback you need. The only kind of feedback that is helpful right now is feedback that is relevant to the changes you're asked to make to your newly assembled ELS in this chapter: keeping your ELS tidy, making sure it's in chronological order, making sure realizations are in the right place, clarifying confusion, filling holes, and reversing overarching old patterns. Any feedback that isn't relevant to the instructions in this chapter (such as grammar suggestions, or pointing out that the end of the story doesn't read like a story—it won't yet) will *not* be helpful, and can even be deflating. Sharing the story of your life, especially in such a raw and unpolished form, is an incredibly vulnerable act, and it's imperative that the person providing feedback is sensitive to that fact, while providing *only* the right kind of feedback.

Chapter 9 ELS Written Exercise

Before you begin, create a sacred, comfortable space to work. Turn off your devices and make sure you won't be interrupted for at least an hour. Read your ELS Intention aloud, and update it, if needed. Then, complete the following:

1. Create a new document titled, *My ELS* (and include today's date in the title).

2. Assemble your ELS, using The Instructions for Using the Copy-and-Paste ELS Template.

3. Edit your ELS, using the Instructions for Basic Edits to Your ELS.

4. Spend some time reversing old patterns that you see manifesting in your writing.

5. Have a trusted friend or writing partner provide you with feedback to ensure that you followed the instructions for this ELS Written Exercise.

6. Add any new breakthroughs or results that you experience while assembling and editing your ELS to the Breakthroughs and Results area of your *My ELS* document, beginning with the date they occurred.

---

in the bank

Visit www.TheELSResourceBank.com to download a printable version of the *Chapter 9 ELS Written Exercise,* which includes the instructions from this chapter that you'll need to complete your exercise.

Ten
Mastering Your Messages

Life is what we make it, always has been, always will be.

—ANAÏS NIN

In the introduction to this book, we talked about how your story contains messages that dictate what's possible for you, and that your thoughts are always in alignment with those messages. In this chapter, you'll identify the Old Messages that are currently ruling over the story of your life, preventing you from having what you need and want, and then evolve them into New Messages that direct your mind to generate thoughts that support the realization of your Greatest Dreams.

Messages are ideas about the nature of reality that are conveyed through story, such as, *Life is like a box of chocolates: you never know what you're going to get.* All stories carry messages—both explicit and implied—and those messages can be uplifting or depressing, healing or harmful, liberating or enslaving. Like perspective itself, messages are inherently fluid and alterable, and you can find evidence for *any* message to be true. However, because stories use a powerful combination of logic and emotion, the messages they carry don't *feel* changeable—they feel like law.

When I was a little girl, my mom refused to take me to the movie *E.T. the Extra-Terrestrial,* because she assumed that it would give me nightmares. But that was because the only messages she'd ever received about aliens were negative. Thankfully, because so many people were talking about how different *E.T.* was, she changed her mind and took me to see it, and an alien stole my heart.

I wasn't alone. *E.T.* conveyed positive messages about aliens so masterfully that it completely changed the way an entire generation thought and felt about them. This ability to deliver powerful New Messages that people absorb and accept as fact, without even being aware of it, is the storyteller's superpower.

As the author of your own story, you have this same superpower. You have the ability to incorporate New Messages into your story that completely change the way you think and feel about what's possible for you—no matter what has happened in your past.

The Origins of Old Messages

Old Messages are heavy, negative statements about the nature of reality and your place inside of it that are woven throughout your story, preventing you from having what you need and want. The Old Messages in your story are often confused with "facts," simply because they were unconsciously written into your story when you were a child—based on things that happened to you—before you were able to process your experiences objectively. When you were a child, everything that happened to you seemed like it was about you. And once your mind—through your child-like perspective—found even a small amount of evidence for why an Old Message was true for you, that message got locked down in your story. You then unconsciously began to look for, and find, *more* supporting evidence for that Old Message. Like a snowball rolling down a hill, the Old Message gained more evidence, power, and momentum as it rolled through time, until it became an irrefutable truth in your mind.

It's common for Old Messages to make their way into your story, in early childhood, through books, movies, TV shows, and other forms of media. One popular Old Message that shows up prominently in Disney films, like *Cinderella* and *Sleeping Beauty,* is, *True love always happens at first sight.* Just by watching these films, that Old Message may have slipped into your story unconsciously. Once absorbed by your story, this Old Message would likely cause you to over-attach to romantic partners, before even having the opportunity to get to know them. At the same time, this Old Message could cause you to *reject* romantic partners with whom you *would* be compatible, simply because sparks didn't fly when they first caught your eye. Thankfully, the source of this Old Message is starting to shift. In the recent Disney movie *Frozen,* for example, Elsa tells her sister, "You can't marry a man you just met." Essentially, Elsa is implying the New Message that, *True love takes time to grow.*

There's a feedback loop between the messages in your story and the messages in our culture's stories. The process of evolving Old Messages into New Messages is similar, whether it's happening in our collective stories or our personal ones. The more conscious you become of the messages in your own story, the more easily you will see the messages that come your way through books, films, and TV shows, and the less susceptible you will be to unconsciously absorbing messages that don't serve you.

Wherever they come from, it's important to understand that Old Messages aren't *bad*—they're an important part of your story's evolution. They may be holding you back now, but they actually served you for a time. And they'll serve you in this chapter too, because you wouldn't be able to create your empowering New Messages if not for the Old Messages from which they'll evolve.

Your Message List

In your ELS Written Exercise for this chapter, you'll create your Message List, which consists of three essential sets of messages: three Old

Messages and three New Messages that will replace them. Your Message List may be long at first—that's normal! Just marry similar sets of messages and distill your list until you have only three essential sets of messages: those that feel like they hold the greatest power to change your life *right now.*

When my client Holly first completed her Message List in this chapter, she had *ten* sets of messages and needed help distilling them down to three. When I read her Message List, I could see that several of the Old Messages on her list weren't actually Old Messages, but were rather things that she told herself because of a deeper Old Message at play. She listed Old Messages such as: *You don't even know what you want; You should just be grateful for what you have; You can't break out of your station in life; You'll never stick with it;* and *You can't do it.* But each of these statements were actually just things that she told herself to sabotage her dream of becoming a solo-singer (and stay put in her band as a back-up singer). The underlying, dominant Old Message was, *I have to stop myself from doing what I want to do.* The process of essentializing her messages allowed us to find the Old Messages that were truly preventing her from having what she wanted and turn them around. Her Message List became:

Old Message: *I have to stop myself from doing what I want to do.*

New Message: *I encourage myself to have dreams and go for them.*

Old Message: *There's no room for what I need and want.*

New Message: *What I need and want is very important.*

Old Message: *I'm going to fail.*

New Message: *I'll always succeed if I just keep practicing.*

You can expect to experience the same thing when crafting your Message List. At first, you'll have way too many messages, and upon deeper examination, you'll find that many of the statements that you *thought* were Old Messages are actually just things that you do or tell yourself because of a deeper, more dominant message that needs to be transformed. After distilling your Message List down to three essential sets, you'll feel so much better, just like Holly did, and you'll be excited about the idea of bringing the New Messages into your ELS, so they can take root.

Instructions for Identifying Your Old Messages

Here's how to find the Old Messages in your ELS:

1. LOOK FOR EXPLICIT OLD MESSAGES.

Some Old Messages will be simple and easy to find, because they're written verbatim in your ELS, right after the experiences that seem to provide evidence for why they're true. For example, you may follow a heartbreaking account of how you were cheated on for the third time with the Old Message, *Men suck.* Or you may follow a grisly description of a particularly rough chapter in your life with the Old Message, *Life is hard.* Or you may follow a series of traumatic events with the Old Message, *Bad things always happen to me.* Any such negative, overarching statements about the story of your life that feel like "facts" you need to resign yourself to are contenders for the three essential Old Messages on your Message List.

2. LOOK FOR IMPLIED OLD MESSAGES.

Some Old Messages in your story are implied rather than stated, so you have to do a little digging and contemplation to find them. Whenever you notice a negative repeating pattern in your story, ask yourself what Old Message is held inside of it. I noticed a prominent pattern in my client Melissa's story of things taking a sudden turn for the worse, right after things started getting better.

She wrote about the time that she was excited to go on vacation with her family, because they'd never been able to afford a vacation before, right before describing how they had to return home early because their dog was injured in a fishing accident. Then she wrote about how excited her family was to buy a new house, which turned out to have a laundry list of unforeseen problems. The hidden Old Message in her story was, *Every time things start to get good, the other shoe drops.*

3.   **CONSIDER THE MEANING YOU HAVE ASSIGNED TO NEGATIVE EXPERIENCES.**

Old Messages can also make their way into your story through negative assumptions you make about yourself as a result of bad things that have happened to you. If you see a memory in your ELS that feels heavy and significant, ask yourself, *What negative belief do I have about myself, or about life, as a result of this experience?* One of my clients had this line in his ELS about his first memory: *When I was two, my mom left me alone in the family station wagon, which then rolled down the driveway and into the road.* I knew that there had to be a hidden Old Message connected to that experience, because it was his first memory, and also because it was significant, negative, and scary. I asked him what negative belief he imagined he had about himself as a result of the experience, and his response revealed the hidden Old Message that, *I am easily forgotten.*

4.   **LOOK FOR PLACES WHERE YOU CONTRADICT YOURSELF.**

If you notice a place in your ELS where you contradict something you wrote elsewhere in the story, that's a sign of a hidden Old Message. For example, let's say your parents had an unhealthy marriage and you describe their relationship in a way that makes marriage sound like a prison sentence. Then, toward the end of your story, you describe your dream of marrying your soulmate and living happily ever after. The Old Message you'd be unconsciously telling yourself about your parents' marriage would be at odds with the message that you'd be *trying* to tell yourself about what marriage could be for you. In this case, it would be important to identify the Old Message you're telling yourself about marriage, which might be, *Marriage is a prison sentence*, so that it can evolve into a New Message that supports your dream, like, *Marriage is a liberating blessing.*

5. **REVISIT YOUR CHAPTER 4 ELS WRITTEN EXERCISE RESPONSES.**

Many of the Old Messages in your ELS will make their way into your story through your parents' influence. Look back at your ELS Written Exercise for chapter 4 and ask yourself if you see any Old Messages in your responses that are connected to repeating patterns in your ELS. For example, if your dad didn't meet your need for attention, because he rarely spent time with you, you may have come to believe the Old Message that, *I have to work really hard to get attention,* and thus attract romantic partners who also rarely spend time with you. Or if your mom often said, "What is wrong with you?!" you may have adopted the Old Message that, *Something is wrong with me.*

6. **PAY ATTENTION TO MEMORIES THAT COME TO MIND AS YOU EDIT.**

Sometimes as you're working on your Message List, a memory will come to mind of an experience that isn't currently in your ELS, because it carries a powerful Old Message inside of it that your mind wants you to become aware of. This happened to me once: My dream was to make a bigger impact with the work that I do, and while I was working on my Message List, I suddenly remembered the time that Mrs. Bivens, my middle school cheer-leading coach, said to me, "You don't have what it takes to be a leader." Her words became an implied Old Message in my story that, *I don't have what it takes to be a leader.* This Old Message unconsciously directed my thoughts and influenced my actions for decades—causing me to gravitate toward situations where my leadership skills were judged or overpowered. When I realized that it was operating behind the scenes in my story, I evolved it into, *I'm a natural leader.* So, if seemingly random memories arise while working on your Message List, please take the time to reflect on what Old Message your mind is trying to reveal to you.

7. **NOTICE ANY OLD MESSAGES THAT YOU ABSORBED FROM POPULAR CULTURE.**

If you mention a story from popular culture in your ELS that had a big impact on you, it's likely that you wrote about it because an Old Message from that story was adopted into your own. Ask yourself, *What Old Message from this story might have become absorbed into mine?* For example, one of my clients wrote in her ELS about watching *Les Misérables* on Broadway when she was six years old. She resonated so strongly with the character Éponine, who didn't get to be with the man she loved, that she adopted the Old Message that was governing Éponine's story into her own story, *I don't get to be with the man I love.*

8. **LOOK FOR OLD MESSAGES IN YOUR FAIRY TALE FREEWRITE.**

Your Chapter 7 ELS Written Exercise is a great place to look for potential Old Messages. Ask yourself what Old Message was governing the main character in your Fairy Tale Freewrite (who represents you) before overcoming their challenge. For example, one of my clients wrote her Fairy Tale Freewrite about a monster-man that she was able to free herself from using magic. The Old Message in her Fairy Tale Freewrite, which was also present in her ELS, was, *Men are monsters.* Using the instructions in the following section, she was able to transform that Old Message into the New Message that, *Men are angels.*

Instructions for Crafting Your New Messages

Even though Old Messages feel like irrefutable truths, they can change in an instant. For each Old Message you identify, you will create an equally powerful and opposite New Message to reverse it. Your New Messages will describe reality as you *would like it to be*, and thus represent a very different reality from the one you've been experiencing.

1. WRITE YOUR NEW MESSAGES IN PRESENT, POSITIVE LANGUAGE.

Make sure that you write your New Messages in present, positive language, as if they are *already* true. For example, if your Old Message is, *I'm unlovable*, your New Message would be, *I am lovable*, rather than, *I want to be lovable*, or, *One day I will feel lovable*. If your Old Message is, *I'm always alone*, your New Message would be, *I am infinitely loved and supported*, rather than, *One day I might not be alone.*

2. CONVERT YOUR OLD MESSAGES WORD-FOR-WORD.

The best way to create a New Message is by converting its Old Message counterpart word-for-word. For example, if your Old Message is, *Life is hard*, an ideal New Message would be, *Life is easy* or *Life is fun*, because the subjects are the same and the sentence structures are parallel. Similarly, if your Old Message is, *Money brings out the worst in people*, an ideal New Message would be, *Money brings out the best in people.*

3. **MAKE SURE YOUR NEW MESSAGE IS THE SAME LENGTH AS YOUR OLD MESSAGE.**

When converting your Old Messages, it's common to come up with New Messages that are a lot longer and wordier than the Old Messages they're meant to replace, which makes the New Message less powerful. For example, you might try to replace an Old Message like, *Men suck,* with a New Message like, *Men can be okay if you are able to find one who's trustworthy.* But an ideal New Message is simply, *Men are wonderful.*

4. **MAKE SURE YOUR NEW MESSAGE IS MORE COMPELLING THAN YOUR OLD MESSAGE.**

It's important to compare the power of each of your Old Messages with the power of their New Message replacements, before considering your Message List complete. For example, the Old Message, *I'm doomed for failure,* is very powerful, and your New Message needs to be even more powerful to reverse it. A New Message like, *I'm capable of succeeding,* wouldn't be strong enough. To fully reverse, *I'm doomed for failure,* you would need a New Message like, *I'm destined for success.*

5. **STRETCH YOURSELF TO WRITE YOUR ABSOLUTE IDEAL.**

In order for a New Message to change your life in a positive way, it has to describe a reality that is *different* from the one you've been living. You'll know that you've successfully achieved that when your New Message feels exciting, but untrue. Anytime I'm working with a client and they feel stuck coming up with a New Message, I ask them, "If a genie fell from the sky right now and could grant your any wish, what New Message would you ask for, to rule over the story of your life?" When you answer that question honestly, you'll have your ideal New Message every time.

6. **MAKE SURE THE OLD MESSAGE COULD NOT COEXIST WITH THE NEW MESSAGE.**

You will know that a New Message is able to fully counteract an Old Message when it would be impossible for the Old Message and New Message to be true at the same time. One of my clients had an Old Message that, *Others have control over me.* In reversing that, she came up with a New Message that, *I have control over myself.* And while that New Message is on the same subject, is the same length, and is a direct opposite of the Old Message, both the Old Message and the New Message *could* be true at the same time. We talked it through and came up with the New Message that, *Nothing is more powerful than my connection to myself,* which described a reality in which it was impossible for anyone to have more control over her than she did. When a New Message fully names your ideal in this way, your Old Message can simply no longer be true.

7. **DON'T BE LIMITED BY CULTURAL NORMS.**

Just as you have the power to upgrade your parental modeling through story, you have the power to upgrade your *cultural* modeling through story. And evolving the messages in your story is, in my opinion, the most powerful way to do that. There are indigenous peoples around the world who live by completely different rules than people in our culture do—ideals like, *Everyone is accepted and lovable, We honor one another's needs,* and *People are good.* We can look to, and emulate, those aspects of their model that feel right and good through the creation of New Messages—no matter how impossible it may seem for those New Messages to be true in *our* culture. If a New Message feels good to you, and you would *like* it to be true, it *can* be and it deserves a home in your story.

Joseph Campbell named his book *The Hero with a Thousand Faces* to highlight the fact that each one of us is living out the same overarching story in their own unique way. When helping clients clarify their Message Lists, I'm often fascinated by this truth, which is evident in the parallel messages I see from one client to another, even as the stories that contain those messages are unique. Because of our inherent interconnection, you can benefit from looking at the work that others have already done on their own messages. In the ELS Resource Bank, I provide you with a list of common Old and New Messages that you can adopt—word-for-word or adapted—if they resonate and feel relevant to your own story.

in the bank

Visit www.TheELSResourceBank.com to find *25 of the Most Common Message Sets.*

Path Skipping in Chapter 10

When completing your ELS Written Exercise, it's common to wonder, *What difference will these fantasy New Messages make? It's not like my story could ever prove that they're true.* If that happens, just know that it's completely normal to question this exercise, and complete the exercise anyway! As you start creating your ideal New Messages, your mind will, all on its own, naturally start to look for and find evidence for how these "fantasy New Messages" are actually true.

Another way to skip off the path is to focus on "themes" instead of messages. Themes are topics that show up again and again in your story. We don't focus on themes in the ELS Method because doing so is a trap, *and* it's unnecessary. Themes themselves are neutral, but it's the messages attached to them that hold power over you and your story. While it's tempting (and extremely common) to run with a theme while editing your ELS, such as heart language and imagery, doing so won't change your life. However, evolving the Old Message that's attached to that theme, such as, *Following my heart is foolish,* into a New Message like, *Following my heart is wise,* would have a powerful impact on your life.

Chapter 10 ELS Written Exercise

Before you begin, create a sacred, comfortable space to work. Turn off your devices and make sure you won't be interrupted for at least an hour. Open your *My ELS* document, read your ELS Intention and update it if needed, and then complete the following:

1. Make a list of the Old Messages in your ELS using the Instructions for Identifying Your Old Messages, under the header "Message List."

2. For each Old Message on your list, create a New Message to counteract it, following the Instructions for Crafting Your New Messages.

3. Combine and distill your Message List until you have three essential sets.

4. Have a trusted friend or writing partner provide you with feedback on your Message List, making sure that you followed both sets of instructions from this chapter.

5. Add any significant breakthroughs or results that you experience under the Breakthroughs and Results area of your *My ELS* document.

in the bank

Visit www.TheELSResourceBank.com to download a printable version of the *Chapter 10 ELS Written Exercise*, which includes all of the instructions from this chapter that you'll need to complete your exercise.

Eleven

Weaving and
Balancing Your ELS

*If you have built castles in the air, your work need not be lost;
that is where they should be. Now put the foundations under them.*

—HENRY DAVID THOREAU

In chapter 9, we talked about how assembling the first draft of your ELS was like taking the first step toward creating a piece of Kintsugi art, where the "broken pieces" of your story get put back together again. In this chapter, your Old and New Messages will become the ribbons of gold, woven throughout your ELS, that hold it together and transform your story into an inspiring work of art that propels you into the future of your dreams.

It may sound counter-intuitive that the "gold" in your ELS includes your Old Messages, but it does. Your Old Messages are a very important part of your ELS. The younger parts of you will always relate to your Old Messages and if you just erase them, those younger parts of you will feel alienated and abandoned. By telling the story of how your Old Messages *evolve* into your New Messages, you provide those younger parts of yourself with a lifeline that includes them in the process of realizing your Greatest Dreams. The evolution of your messages from old to new, through story, *is* the gold in your ELS.

Instructions for Weaving Your Messages

In your ELS Written Exercise for this chapter, you'll use editing techniques to weave each set of messages on your Message List through the beginning and middle of your ELS. The beginning of your ELS includes all content leading up to your Story Core, the middle includes all Story Core content, and the end includes everything that follows. You don't have to be a screenwriter, playwright, or novelist to understand, or successfully use, any of these editing techniques. With a little practice, these techniques will become fun, simple, and second-nature to you.

1. **ESTABLISH YOUR OLD MESSAGES.**

   There are two steps to establishing an Old Message: state it word-for-word and then convey it with a vignette, or a mini-story, to provide context. You need to mention each of your Old Messages in the part of your story when you first learned them, which—with rare exceptions—will be in the beginning of your ELS, before your Story Core. When establishing an Old Message, you may find that you already have a vignette in your ELS to support it. If so, great! But if not, ask yourself, *What short story from my past communicates how and why I started believing this Old Message?* Then write the vignette that comes to mind into your ELS, chronologically.

   If your Old Message is, *Life is unfair,* you could establish it by writing the vignette: *My sister always got new clothes, and I got her hand-me-downs. Life is unfair.* If your Old Message is, *I'm a black sheep,* you could establish it by writing: *I'm a black sheep. At family gatherings I used to sit in the corner wondering if I'd secretly been adopted, as people wore hideous sweaters and made bad jokes.*

Here's an example to help you understand how establishing Old Messages in the beginning of your ELS will lend strength to your New Messages later on in the process. Let's say your Old Message is, *I can't grow up*, and your New Message is, *I'm a powerful grown woman*. If you simply removed all the content from your ELS about the Old Message, the New Message would feel weird and out of context when you mention it later in the story. Your Ideal Reader would wonder, *Why does she need to proclaim that she's a grown woman?* But if the Old Message were properly established in the beginning of your ELS, your New Message (which will be mentioned in the end of your story, never in the beginning) will make complete sense and feel compelling to your Ideal Reader, in the end.

2. EVIDENCE YOUR NEW MESSAGES.

After you've established each of your three Old Messages in the beginning of your ELS, you'll provide evidence for each of your three New Messages, in the middle of your story (your Story Core), or shortly thereafter. You'll evidence your New Messages with empowering vignettes that I call Mini Power Stories. You'll write a couple lines describing each Mini Power Story—chronologically in your ELS—in a way that supports the New Message, without yet stating the New Message explicitly (that will happen later, in your Ideal Ending).

Remember, you can *always* find supporting evidence in your own personal history for any New Message to be true. One of the easiest ways to find evidence for your New Messages is to revisit your List of Positive Memories from chapter 6. You can also simply ask yourself, *What examples from my own personal history prove that this New Message is true?* Asking yourself this question will cause memories to spontaneously arise that can serve as Mini Power

Stories. The potential Story Core freewrites that you crafted in chapter 6 can also be distilled down and turned into Mini Power Stories that support your New Messages.

Your Story Core itself will also serve as evidence for at least one of your New Messages, if not all of them. If your Story Core *doesn't* feel supportive of any of your New Messages, you'll need to either revise your Message List until at least one of your New Messages is evidenced by your Story Core, or consider choosing a different Story Core that *does* support one or more of your New Messages.

One of my clients had an Old Message that, *It's really hard to get acting work,* and a New Message that, *Acting work comes easily to me.* Her New Message felt impossible at first, but when she asked herself what evidence she could find to support it, her mind automatically started coming up with all the times in her life that acting jobs *had* come to her easily—and it was a long list. Yet, none of the abundant evidence to support her New Message was currently in her story (which is *why* she was always focusing on how hard it was to get acting work). Once she added the supporting evidence for her New Message, the power of her Old Message melted away, and she got more acting gigs in the following week than she had gotten at one time, ever before.

The more Mini Power Stories you integrate into your ELS, the more your mind will naturally look for—and find—additional evidence for your New Messages. In turn, Source will send you even more experiences that provide further evidence still. Like snowballs rolling down a hill, your New Messages will continually amass more evidence and grow stronger with time.

3. EDIT YOUR MESSAGE LIST AS YOU WEAVE.

In the last chapter, you largely worked on your messages, independent of your story. As a result, when you're weaving your Message Sets throughout your ELS, you will realize that some of them don't "fit" your story as much as you thought they did. If you find it difficult to establish an Old Message, it's because it's not actually an Old Message, but rather, a pattern you fall into, or something you say to yourself as a subconscious way to stay beholden to a deeper, hidden Old Message.

My client Jana had an Old Message on her list that, *I'm not enough,* and a corresponding New Message that, *I am more than enough.* However, while she was trying to think of a vignette to establish her Old Message, a vignette came to mind that supported an entirely different Old Message that wasn't even on her list—an Old Message that was actually significantly tied to her Greatest Current Challenge. A boy at her school (who was popular, but not very hard-working) wanted to join her team for a project. When she spoke up for herself by saying, "You just want me to do all the work," he got angry and told all of his friends to stop talking to her. The Old Message tied to *that* vignette was, *If I stand up for myself, I'll get kicked out of the herd.* After replacing the first Old Message with this more essential one, Jana was able to evolve it into a New Message that was much more relevant to her story and her Greatest Dreams, which was, *I am embraced by my herd when I stand up for myself.*

This dance between clarifying the messages on your Message List and weaving them into your story is a vitally important part of using the ELS Method. You can update your messages as you edit, either by re-wording them or by replacing them entirely. In the end, the messages on your list will be the same as the messages in your ELS—word-for-word—and the more you embrace this dance, the greater your results will be.

Instructions for Balancing Your ELS

The balancing techniques you'll use in this stage of the ELS Method will reveal and address the interconnected imbalances in your story and your life. Several years ago, a couple of friends read my ELS and reflected to me that Justin, the man I was dating, took up *way* too much space in my story. I knew intellectually that they were right, and that I should follow the rules of my own method—which said that no part of your story should be longer than your Story Core—but I was so attached to every sentence about Justin that I couldn't bring myself to cut any one of them.

My resistance to paring down this Trouble Spot in my story made me realize that I was hiding something important from myself. After repeatedly trying—and failing—to distill the Justin parts of my story, I desperately pleaded with my story out loud, "Please just show me the truth! I'm ready now and I want to see it." Within minutes, I had a breakthrough where I realized that I was much more invested in this man than he was in me. It wasn't a particularly fun realization, but it was definitely an empowering one. Then suddenly, it became really easy to take most of the content about Justin out of my story. After Justin faded out of my story, he faded out of my life, as well. So, as you use the following techniques to balance your ELS, be ready to experience significant realizations that will forever change the story of your life.

1. **MAKE SURE THAT YOUR STORY CORE IS THE STAR OF YOUR ELS.**

   Ideally, no single relationship description or experience in your ELS will be longer than your Story Core. So, if you notice any area of your story that *is* longer than your Story Core, spend some time distilling it until it is *shorter* than your Story Core; balancing your ELS in this way will ensure that your Story Core is the "star" of your ELS and that it uplifts you as it's meant to.

2. **DISTILL THE CONTENT THAT SUPPORTS YOUR OLD MESSAGES.**

After establishing your Old Messages, you'll notice that you still have lots of additional content, later in your ELS, that shows how your Old Messages lived on and dominated the story of your life after you learned them. It's important to keep such Old Message content in your ELS, but to distill it down to only what is essential. So, for example, if you have an Old Message that, *Nice guys are boring*, and your story describes in detail three times you got bored with a nice guy and left him for a jerk, you can keep the details surrounding the *most significant* of the three relationships, and then cut all but a couple of sentences about the other times you got bored with a nice guy and left him for a jerk. Or, you could simply remove all but one of the relationship descriptions and then add a line like, *I kept repeating this pattern for the next 20 years.*

3. **IDENTIFY AND DISTILL TROUBLE SPOTS.**

A Trouble Spot is any part of your ELS that feels heavy, confusing, or excessively long, and it's almost always difficult to clarify and pare down. The easiest way to distill a Trouble Spot is to use what I call "The Expand and Distill Technique." First, you'll write *more* about that Trouble Spot, describing it in *greater* detail, until you experience a breakthrough in your awareness (which may involve a hidden Old Message) that dissolves your confusion. Then, you'll distill the Trouble Spot back down to no more than a paragraph, since you'll no longer need most of the content that was necessary to arrive at that breakthrough. Leave only what's essential.

4. **REVISIT ELS LETTERS, AS NEEDED.**

If you still find it difficult to distill a Trouble Spot, you may have unfinished business with someone who's involved with that part of your story. If so, it's best to write a set of ELS Letters with that person, before trying to distill the Trouble Spot further. If you've *already* written ELS Letters with that person, you may need to write an addendum to that set of letters. Ask yourself, *Is the way in which this person hurt me or what they modeled (that is showing up in my Trouble Spot) specifically addressed in my ELS Letters with them?* If not, write a new, mini-set of ELS Letters with that person, addressing only what was left out of the first set of ELS Letters, following the instructions in chapter 5. After you've completed (or refreshed) your ELS Letters with the person involved in your Trouble Spot, it will be much easier to distill.

5. **EXPLORE HOW THE CHALLENGE IN THE TROUBLE SPOT PREPARED YOU FOR YOUR DREAMS.**

Another helpful way to distill a Trouble Spot is to ask yourself, *How has the challenge I'm experiencing in this Trouble Spot uniquely prepared me to realize my Greatest Dreams?* Write the answer to that question in the Breakthroughs and Results area of your ELS. Doing so will make it easier to bring the Trouble Spot into balance.

6. **IMPROVE HONESTY.**

As we discussed in chapter 2, you could write a million different versions of your story that are all true, and by now, you have an experiential understanding of that truth. The more you edit your ELS, however, the more you'll find that there's a *spectrum* of truth. Any moment of your life can be described in various true ways, but certain descriptions will be *more* true than others. And the truest description will always be the one that is most concise, direct, and empowering. For example, I've had multiple clients write about a time when they were sexually assaulted, but they wrote those experiences as if the sex had been consensual. When they had the courage to write the truest version of the experience—that they had been assaulted—they put an end to the painful and confusing cycle of self-blame.

7. **COLOR-CODE YOUR MESSAGES.**

Color-coding is a helpful way to make imbalances and Trouble Spots in your story more visible, so you can easily address them. You can use colored pencils on a printed version of your ELS, or use the highlighting function in a digital version of your ELS, to visually measure the amount of space you give to different experiences in your story. More specifically, you can use color-coding to easily see how much space you give to content that relates to your Old Messages, as compared to evidence that supports your New Messages. I recommend using two different shades of the same color for each Message Set—a darker shade to highlight Old Message content and a lighter shade to highlight New Message evidence. Just be sure to touch on each message set at least once in the beginning of your ELS and once in the middle. In the next chapter, you'll touch on each message set again when you create your Ideal Ending.

Path Skipping in Chapter 11

When one of my clients was in this stage of the process, it suddenly landed for her that there's a direct connection between her story and her thoughts. And even though the instructions said otherwise, she took everything out of her story that felt heavy and negative—including her Old Messages and all related content. Initially, she felt better, and even manifested several immediate career advancements, which she attributed to the ELS Method. But then her progress plateaued.

She had "whitewashed" her story by deliberately concealing everything that felt unpleasant, and in doing so, she had inadvertently placed a limit on how far her New Messages could take her. As I mentioned in the beginning of this chapter, there are parts of you that *need* your Old Messages in your story. Including your Old Messages in your ELS will ensure that your mind quickly realigns with your New Messages, all on its own, any time it momentarily drops back into your Old Messages. So, in order for her Old Messages to evolve, she *had* to include them in her story, and once she did, her career moved to an entirely new level.

Your Old Messages might feel like they're written in stone, but they're actually just well-rehearsed. They've had a lot of time to amass content that makes them feel true. On the other hand, your New Messages are brand new and have not yet taken root in your story. But once they do, they will gain strength and momentum in the same way your Old Messages did. As you complete these two final chapters, the power of your Old Messages will transfer over to your New Messages, and your New Messages will become the new driving force in the story of your life.

Lastly, you may skip off the path by waiting to move on to chapter 12 until your ELS Written Exercise in this chapter is completed perfectly... but that will never happen! After crafting your Ideal Ending in chapter 12, you'll return to your ELS Written Exercise for this chapter, and feel much more satisfied with its completion at that time.

Chapter 11 ELS Written Exercise

Before you begin, create a sacred, comfortable space to work. Turn off your devices and make sure you won't be interrupted for at least an hour. Open your *My ELS* document, read your ELS Intention and update it if needed, and then complete the following:

1. Weave your messages into your ELS, using the Instructions for Weaving Your Messages.

2. Balance your ELS, using the Instructions for Balancing Your ELS.

3. Have a trusted friend or writing partner provide you with feedback to ensure you followed the instructions for this ELS Written Exercise.

4. Write down any breakthroughs or results you experience in this stage of the process in the Breakthroughs and Results section of your *My ELS* document, beginning the entry with the date.

in the bank — Visit www.TheELSResourceBank.com to download a printable version of the *Chapter 11 ELS Written Exercise,* which includes the instructions from this chapter that you'll need to complete your exercise.

Twelve
Writing Your Ideal Ending

Claim your birthright… give this story a happy ending.

—FROM THE FILM *KUBO*

As we discussed in the introduction to this book, you can't just write a new ending to your old story—doing so would be like trying to put the head of a unicorn on the body of a slug. But by this point in the process, you no longer have an "old story." Step-by-step, you've broken down your old story and transmuted its content and perspective in such a way that your narrative no longer resembles a slug, but a unicorn! And now, that unicorn is ready for its head. In this chapter, you'll craft the "head of your unicorn," or the Ideal Ending of your ELS—an inspiring ending that lifts you up and makes you feel certain that your Greatest Dreams will come true.

Your Dream Continuum and How it Affects Your Mind

Your Dream Continuum is a river of energy, a flow of consciousness that moves through your ELS—and thus your mind and life—leading you towards your Ideal Ending. When you follow the instructions for the ELS Method, everything in your life, mind, and story will lead back to that "river."

When your ELS is complete, each negative past experience in your story will connect to an Old Message, which will then evolve into a corresponding New Message, with plenty of supporting evidence for why it's true, and everything will lead back to your Ideal Ending. Your mind will naturally surrender to this beautiful river of consciousness that supports your dreams, generating thoughts that go along with that flow.

In the preface, I talked about my realization that I needed to build a bridge between my past and my ideal future, and how creating that bridge, by writing the first draft of my ELS, immediately began to change my life in significant ways. However, about a year after writing my first ELS, I was feeling stuck when it came to manifesting a successful coaching practice. I revisited my ELS to see if I could find the source of why I was stuck, and discovered that my dream of having a successful coaching practice wasn't even in my story! Within days of adding the phrase, *I look forward to having a successful coaching practice,* to my Ideal Ending, a friend gave me an extensive video training program about online marketing strategies that could help me achieve that goal. That's how quickly simple additions to your Ideal Ending can bring about positive changes in your life after your ELS is complete!

What happened next, however, felt even more significant. As I dove into studying these online marketing strategies, it quickly became apparent that I was going to have to really "put myself out there," and that idea terrified me. I thought, *How am I ever going to do this?* Before having written my ELS, my mind would have shown me a montage of all the bad things that would happen if I did what scared me, and put myself out there, and it would have taken a lot of heavy lifting to get my mind back to a positive place. But because I'd already written my ELS, my mind started showing me evidence, all on its own, that I was not only capable of doing things that scared me, but that it was something I'd historically loved to do! My mind showed me all the times I'd done things that had initially scared me, like riding motocross, jumping horses, and traveling to other countries by myself—things that enriched my life and worked out well for me. It was so sweet to notice my mind working *for* me instead of against me, without any effort on my part at all.

When I started sharing the ELS Method with others, I was delighted to find that my experience was *not* an anomaly. Everyone I've led through the process has experienced this mind-changing phenomenon, beginning with Holly, the first person with whom I shared the process. Holly had been working abroad when she applied to live in a well-known artists' community house, but unfortunately, they rejected her application. Before having written her ELS, Holly had always fallen into depression when she didn't get what she wanted, thinking thoughts like, *Nothing ever works out for me.* But because she'd now written her ELS, which was filled with evidence for how things actually *are* always working out for her (even when it may not appear that way at first), Holly responded to this "rejection" in a completely different way. She felt at peace with their decision and thought, *I guess there's somewhere even better for me to live out there.* Shortly thereafter, an acquaintance invited Holly to stay in her home on a beautiful island and it was actually a much better living situation for her, because it was quieter and better suited for all the creative writing she was going to do.

Once you've completed your ELS, you can expect to experience the same: your thoughts will flow with the river of consciousness set forth in your Dream Continuum, your mind will naturally align with the new story of your life, and you will be predisposed to find the blessing inside of any challenge you may face.

Instructions for Crafting Your Ideal Ending

Currently, the end of your ELS is dangling; it ends somewhat randomly, wherever your Five-Page Freewrite ended, or with a memory that you added in chapter 11. Now, it's time to give your ELS a proper ending. While crafting your Ideal Ending is a fairly simple process, it's also a very powerful one. Once crafted, your Ideal Ending will make you feel more optimistic about your dreams coming true than ever and it will open a portal between the present and the future, where your Greatest Dreams really do come true.

1. **SET THE STAGE.**

   Add a sentence to your ELS, chronologically, about what inspired you to begin using the ELS Method. For example, you might write, *I was feeling so stuck and wanted to finally record my album, when a friend told me about this story process.* Then, follow that sentence with descriptions of the most significant shifts you have experienced, from the *Breakthroughs and Results* section, in the order that you experienced them. Writing about the life-changing benefits of your ELS inside of your ELS will strengthen your Dream Continuum, reinforce your belief in the power of your story, and inspire you to update your ELS in the future so it can help you overcome new challenges just as it helped you to overcome previous challenges in the past.

2. **REFRAME YOUR GREATEST CURRENT CHALLENGE.**

   Next, you'll copy and paste your New Reality Statement (#11 from your chapter 7 ELS Written Exercise) into your Ideal Ending. When you look back, you may be surprised to realize that the ELS Method has already helped you to overcome the challenge inside of your New Reality Statement. If so, yay! Now complete your Chapter 7 ELS Written Exercise again, using the Greatest Current Challenge that you are *now* facing, and copy that *newer* New Reality Statement into your Ideal Ending, instead (you can keep the previous one in your ELS Written Exercises document). Whatever challenge you're now facing, you'll experience a boost of optimism by addressing it with a New Reality Statement. Just be sure to include the Root Experience (that underlies your Greatest Current Challenge) chronologically in your ELS, as you were instructed to do in chapter 9. While the New Reality Statement itself reframes your Greatest Current Challenge, incorporating it in your Ideal Ending will place it securely along your Dream Continuum and reframe it further still—the power of your challenge will weaken and you will grow certain of your ability to overcome it.

3. **FREE YOURSELF TO DIVERGE FROM YOUR PARENTS' STORIES.**

Next, you'll add the sentence, *I can see now that being born to my parents uniquely prepared me to realize my Greatest Dreams.* Then, follow it with your Parental Modeling Upgrade Statements (#24c from your chapter 4 ELS Written Exercise for each parent). If you've already included breakthroughs in your Ideal Ending that communicate the same information that's in your Parental Modeling Upgrade Statements in a different way, you can distill, reword, or cut the Parental Modeling Upgrade Statements to avoid redundancy—but only if you've already included this information elsewhere! In order for the younger aspects of you to feel free to be *less* like your parents in negative ways, you have to provide them with ways to be *more* like your parents in positive ways. Incorporating your Parental Modeling Upgrade Statements into your Ideal Ending will provide you with an internal sense of permission to allow the story of your life to diverge from your parents' stories in whatever ways serve you best.

4. **TURN YOUR MESSAGES AROUND.**

In chapter 11, you established your Old Messages in the beginning of your story. Now, you'll mention each Old Message again, and then reference the experiences in your life (which are already previously described in your ELS) that seemed to reinforce the Old Message. After that, you'll write the corresponding New Message and cite evidence for why it's actually more true than the Old Message.

For example: *For a long time, I told myself, "I have to stay under the radar to be safe"* [Old Message]. *And I did that by staying in friend groups with people who stay small and constantly switching the focus of my career so that I didn't have the opportunity to excel* [examples of how the Old Message lived on for you]. *But the truth is, "I'm actually safest when I'm seen and when I speak my mind"* [New Message]—*just as I've seen when I joined a mastermind group with other powerful women, and when I committed to my niche* [evidence for New Message, which is described previously in your ELS]. Repeat this same formula for each set of messages, pivoting the power from Old Messages to New Messages.

5. **REFLECT ON YOUR ALREADY REALIZED DREAMS, IN WRITING.**

In chapter 9, you made sure that the dreams on your Already Realized Dreams List were included in your ELS, chronologically. Now, you'll incorporate those Already Realized Dreams into your Ideal Ending to further strengthen your Dream Continuum, remind yourself of what a powerful manifestor you are, and increase your faith that your current dreams will also come true. Copy the following statements into your Ideal Ending, and fill in the blanks with your Already Realized Dreams (from #5 in your chapter 8 ELS Written Exercise): *Looking back over my story, I can see that so many of my dreams from the past have come true in greater ways than I could have imagined. Since I was a little kid, I dreamt of _____ and then that dream came true. I dreamt of _____ and I did. For years, I dreamt of _____ and then it happened. I dreamt of _____ and did that, too.* Add as many similar statements as necessary to account for all of your significant Already Realized Dreams. It's important that any Already Realized Dream that you reference in your Ideal Ending is described earlier in your ELS, when it manifested, so that your

Ideal Ending makes sense and has a powerful impact on you.

6. FORESHADOW THE MANIFESTATION OF YOUR GREATEST DREAMS.

Your Ideal Ending, and therefore your entire ELS, will end with a clear and simple foreshadowing of your Greatest Dreams coming true—they are the pinnacle of your Dream Continuum. Copy the following statement into your Ideal Ending, and fill in the blanks with your Greatest Dreams (from #4 in your chapter 8 ELS Written Exercise): *I can see now that even—and especially—when it may not look like it at first, Source really is working everything out beautifully for me right now, and making my Greatest Dreams come true. And from where I am now, I have so much to look forward to. I look forward to _____ and _____. And I look forward to _____, _____, and _____.*

It's very important to include each of the pieces in your Ideal Ending that I just described, but it's also important that they're written in your own voice. So, feel free to play with the words I've provided to make them your own, until your Ideal Ending flows and feels like the way you would say it to a friend.

Strengthen Your ELS

As your ELS becomes even more authentic and empowering, it will have an even stronger positive impact on your mind. One way to strengthen your ELS is to make sure that it "sounds" like you. Read your story aloud and ask yourself, *Is this how I would describe this part of my story to a friend?* If not, change the words in writing to match how you would say them.

When you read your ELS aloud, you may notice places where you write about your dreams with *too much* excitement or attachment. Over-enthusiasm about your dreams can actually push them away by making you feel like it's not natural for your dreams to manifest. One of my clients had this line in her story: *I booked two roles on TV back-to-back and I am now officially a professional actor!!* While booking these two roles was important evidence for supporting her New Message—that she was meant to succeed as an actor—the way in which she worded it made it sound like an exception to the norm. So she changed it to read, *Then I booked two roles on TV back-to-back and became a professional actor.* That subtle yet significant shift in tone went a long way toward normalizing the reality of her success.

Another way to make sure your ELS is authentic and empowering is to pay attention to how each sentence *feels* when you read it aloud. The best phrasing will make you feel lighter and breathe easier. Always let your feelings guide your choices about what to keep, re-word, or remove from your ELS.

In the end, make sure that everything in your ELS is there for a reason: to evolve your messages or to support the manifestation of your dreams. If you're confused about whether or not a particular sentence, paragraph, or memory belongs in your ELS, just ask yourself, *Does it provide context for one of my Old Messages, or evidence for one of my New Messages? Or does it relate in any way to one of my dreams?* If the answer is no, you can cut it or move it to *ELS Overflow.* However, if you feel like removing a memory would offend any aspect of you, it's best to keep it in your ELS—that memory likely just needs to be more securely connected to your Dream Continuum.

Path Skipping in Chapter 12

One sneaky way to skip off the path is by writing your Ideal Ending in a way that presumes your Greatest Dreams *have already* come true. For example, not having yet won an Oscar, but writing, *I just won an Oscar!!* That would be dishonest and therefore unhelpful. In order for your ELS to have a positive impact on your mind, everything inside of it needs to be *true*. Make sure to follow the Instructions for Crafting Your Ideal Ending so that your Greatest Dreams are written as if you know they will come true (not as if they already have), and read like, *I look forward to winning an Oscar one day.*

Another way to skip off the path in this chapter is by not incorporating your most significant breakthroughs and results from using the ELS Method into your ELS. If you were stuck when you started the process in ways that you no longer are—even if you used other methods in conjunction with the story process—it's important to give your ELS proper credit; this will ensure that you return to the ELS Method as needed, so it can continue serving you for life.

Lastly, the main way you may skip off the path in this chapter is by resisting writing your Ideal Ending altogether, simply because it holds the greatest potential to change your life. You *will* feel much more optimistic about your dreams after crafting it! So, if you feel resistant, I implore you to just follow the steps, one-by-one, *or* have your writing partner craft your Ideal Ending for you, in exchange for your crafting theirs—the instructions are simple and you'll have no resistance to crafting them for each other!

Chapter 12 ELS Written Exercise

Before you begin, create a sacred, comfortable space to work. Turn off your devices and make sure you won't be interrupted for at least an hour. Open your *My ELS* document, read your ELS Intention and update it if needed, and then complete the following:

1. Craft your Ideal Ending, using The Instructions for Crafting Your Ideal Ending.

2. Strengthen your ELS by reading it aloud, playing with the wording, and making sure it's written in your own voice. Also, spend some time cutting any extraneous words, sentences or paragraphs that don't relate to your Old and New Messages.

3. Edit your ELS again, using each of the following:

   a. The Instructions for Basic Edits to Your ELS from chapter 9 (you'll need to make sure that your ELS stays tidy, clear and in chronological order as it changes)

   b. The ELS Written Exercise instructions for chapters 10 (your messages will need to be fine-tuned after having made more changes to the story)

   c. The ELS Written Exercise instructions for chapter 11 (your story will then need to be fine-tuned again after having made more changes to the messages)

d. The ELS Written Exercise instructions for chapter 12 (your Ideal Ending will need an update to reflect changes to your messages).

4. Have a trusted friend or writing partner provide you with feedback to ensure that you followed the Instructions for Crafting Your Ideal Ending.

5. Complete ELS Letters with any remaining people on your ELS Letters List.

6. Add any significant breakthroughs or results that you experience under the Breakthroughs and Results area of your *My ELS* document.

in the bank

Visit www.TheELSResourceBank.com to download a printable version of the *Chapter 12 ELS Written Exercise*, which includes the instructions from this chapter that you'll need to complete your exercise.

Epilogue
The Road Ahead

Stories are medicine.

—CLARISSA PINKOLA ESTÉS

Completing your ELS is a major milestone! You've made space in your mind and story for your Greatest Dreams and greatly expanded the bounds of what's possible for you. You've raised the vibration of your story, and now your story will lift you up, in turn. Moving forward, you can expect your dreams to be magically drawn to you.

However, as the next phase of your life unfolds, it's important to remember that your Greatest Dreams will almost always manifest in different ways than you would expect them to. So, if a time comes when it appears as if things are getting *worse* instead of better, if you lose a partner, a job, or a role in a creative project, know that Source is simply making space for something even better—it's delivering your dreams *in disguise*.

You get to choose what your Greatest Dreams are, but *Source* gets to decide how to bring those dreams to life, which is wonderful, because Source has the ultimate, omniscient vantage point for choosing—out of all the available options—the very best manifestation process for you!

And usually, the manifestation of your Greatest Dreams will happen in waves.

For many years, my dream was to return to the Amazon. A number of times, it seemed like that dream was coming true—when I was invited to train as a guide for The Pachamama Alliance (TPA), when I completed that training, when I edited their guide training manual, and then when I was invited to complete my apprenticeship journey as a tour leader. But when, despite my best efforts, my plan to return to the Amazon as a guide for TPA didn't come to fruition, I lost hope.

My faith was restored however, by revisiting my ELS, because my dream of returning to the Amazon was so alive in my Ideal Ending. When I *did* return to the Amazon in 2017, it was under very different circumstances than I had previously imagined. I practically had the entire ecolodge to myself, which was perfect because I spent the next three days crying as I reconnected with the jungle and those aspects of myself that had been missing it so dearly. I was grateful for this unexpected solitude and relieved to not be responsible for leading a tour group at that time. I never imagined my dream unfolding in this way, but after it manifested, I could see how perfect it was—the Divine had clearly been orchestrating the delivery of my dream all along.

Your Essential Life Story will give you an incredibly simple and powerful way to restore your faith whenever you find yourself in doubt—and faith is so essential to the manifestation process! Just read your ELS any time you lose hope in your dreams and it will inspire your mind to see the ways in which what you're experiencing *is* supporting the manifestation of your dreams.

Simply reading your ELS will inspire you, but in the days, weeks, and years to come, there is no limit to the additional number of breakthroughs and results it can bring you if you revisit it regularly for updates. Your ELS is a living, breathing document and it's meant to serve you for life, by evolving *with* you.

As you move forward in life, you'll outgrow your story again and again—like a lobster repeatedly outgrows its shell. As you manifest each of your Greatest Dreams, you'll need to add those successes to your ELS and make space for new dreams. And when life brings you new challenges, such as a breakup, job loss, or illness, incorporating it into your ELS, and connecting it to your Dream Continuum will help you immensely in overcoming it.

Every new phase of life deserves a rewrite. Each time you update your ELS, you'll be surprised by how much you've grown, how far you've advanced, and how easy it is to leverage the work you've already completed to manifest what you want for yourself next. When you make a habit of regularly updating your ELS, it will remain your most powerful, lifelong manifestation tool and become a touchstone for your soul.

And, as we come to the end of the road (for now!), I want to take a moment to thank you for using the ELS Method to transform the story of your life. By expanding your capacity to experience abundance and realize your dreams, you've redirected not only your own path, but the path of humanity itself, so that it leads to a place of greater love, peace, and happiness. You've written your ELS for your own benefit, but because of our inherent, human interconnection, your victories are also our victories. Your dreams are our dreams. Your story, is our story.

in the bank

Visit www.TheELSResourceBank.com to download the *Instructions for Updating Your ELS*.

Once Upon a Time...

There was a beautiful and magical world that became so mired in a haze of darkness and despair that many could neither find its root cause, nor find their way out of its depths.

But one-by-one, as people discovered the magic of healing their stories, the haze was lifted and the world became filled with so much hope and light that heaven and earth became one.

Glossary of Terms

5-PAGE FREEWRITE: a short, yet comprehensive story about your life from birth to present that you'll write in chapter 3 to generate raw content for your ELS; it also provides you with a snapshot of your current unseen psychology so that you can easily see unconscious patterns that you simply can't see in any other way.

ABSENT CATEGORY: one of three categories of relationship that you may fall into with one of your parents, which is categorized by your parent being physically absent from your life (whether through abandonment, estrangement, or death).

ALREADY REALIZED DREAMS LIST: a list of all your dreams from the past that have already come true; used to help you have faith that your currently unrealized dreams will come true, too.

BEST POSSIBLE EULOGY: an imaginary, best-case eulogy that you'll freewrite in chapter 8 to get clear about what you want your legacy to be, what your purpose is, and what your Greatest Dreams are.

BIG DREAMS LIST: a list of dreams that you'll create in chapter 8, which includes everything that you would love to be, do, or have before you die, in any area of your life.

BREAKTHROUGHS AND RESULTS: realizations that you have about the story of your life at any time while using the ELS Method and tangible results that you experience as a result of the process (even if they don't always seem directly related), that are both recorded under the header "Breakthroughs and Results," first in your *ELS Written Exercises* document and later (starting in chapter 9) in your *My ELS* document.

CHALLENGING CATEGORY: one of three categories of relationship that you may fall into with one of your parents, which is categorized by abuse, trauma, neglect, or other intense difficulties.

COMMITMENT STATEMENT: a statement of your commitment to the ELS Method, which describes how often you'll work on your ELS, where you'll write, and from whom you'll receive feedback.

COPY-AND-PASTE ELS TEMPLATE: a template, provided for you in chapter 9, for assembling the first draft of your ELS out of the work you've already completed in previous chapters.

ESSENTIAL LIFE STORY (ELS): a 5-page narrative that you'll assemble in chapter 9, which inspires you to think, feel, and behave in ways that support the magical manifestation of your Greatest Dreams.

ELS INTENTION: a clear, concise statement about what you want to achieve with the ELS Method, which specifically speaks to how you want to experience the process, as well as the internal and external results you would like to manifest.

ELS LETTERS LIST: a list of the people with whom you need to write ELS Letters, which you create in chapter 5.

ELS LETTERS: an exercise for resolving unfinished business that helps you to resolve feelings of anger and sadness due to people having hurt you without making amends and frees you to diverge from your parental modeling in any way that serves you and the realization of your Greatest Dreams.

ELS OVERFLOW: the document that contains excess story content that is more appropriate for a longer version of your story, such as a memoir.

ELS RESOURCE BANK: a free online library, which you can join at www.TheELSResourceBank.com, where you'll find supplemental resources to enhance your ELS journey.

ELS WRITTEN EXERCISES: the document where you'll type up your ELS Written Exercise responses for chapters 1-8, with the exception of chapter 5 (your ELS Letters will be kept in their own separate documents).

EMULATION RESPONSE: when you directly copy your parents' model.

EXPRESSION LETTER: part of the ELS Letters process, in chapter 5, in which you'll write *by hand* all of your feelings toward the person with whom you're completing ELS Letters, in the following four emotional categories: anger, sadness, regret, and appreciation—*in that order.*

FAIRY TALE FREEWRITE: a short story that you will freewrite in chapter 8, which provides you with an energetic blueprint for moving beyond your Greatest Current Challenge through the use of metaphor; the moral of this story will be distilled into one sentence, and integrated into your ELS later.

GREAT CATEGORY: one of three categories of relationship that you may fall into with one of your parents that is categorized by feeling pretty good about your relationship, and like your parent is not the source of any "problems" in your life.

GREATEST CURRENT CHALLENGE: the challenge you're currently facing that most significantly impedes the realization of your Greatest Dreams; this challenge will be reframed in the creation of your New Reality Statement in chapter 7.

GREATEST DREAMS: the dreams that matter most to you, that stood out most prominently in your Best Possible Eulogy.

IDEAL ENDING: the metaphorical "head" of the unicorn that is your new story.

IDEAL READER: the imaginary reader that you'll write for; someone who is empathetic, non-judgmental, and has no previous information about your life or story.

LIST OF POSITIVE MEMORIES: a list of the most positive experiences you can remember, which will help you to choose a Story Core, and will also provide you with potential evidence for your New Messages in chapter 11.

MESSAGE LIST: your list of three essential Old Messages and New Messages, which will live at the top of your *My ELS* document beginning in chapter 10 and become woven throughout your story in chapter 11.

MINI POWER STORIES: positive vignettes from your own personal history that become woven into your ELS in chapter 11 to serve as evidence for why your New Messages are true.

MY ELS: the document that contains the most current version of your Essential Life Story.

NEGATIVE PARENTAL MODELING DISENGAGEMENT FORMULA: a formula that you use when completing Parent Letters (ELS Letters with your parents).

NEW MESSAGES: ideas about the nature of reality that become woven throughout your ELS; ideas that support the realization of your Greatest Dreams.

NEW REALITY STATEMENT: a statement that describes and reframes your Greatest Current Challenge so that you can align with the meaning inside of it and use it as an opportunity for growth.

OLD MESSAGES: ideas in your story about the nature of reality and your place inside of it; ideas that prevent you from having what you need and want (until they become turned into New Messages in chapter 10 and their power is redirected toward those New Messages in chapters 11 and 12).

PARENT FREEWRITES: Five-sentence-long mini versions of your parents' stories that you craft in chapter 4.

PARENT LETTERS: ELS Letters written with your parents (you'll find *Additional Parent Letter Instructions* in the ELS Resource Bank).

PARENTAL MODELING UPGRADE STATEMENTS: declarations of the opportunity inside of having been born to each of your parents that allow you to disengage from the negative aspects of their modeling while, at the same time, align more powerfully with the positive aspects of their modeling.

PATH SKIPPING: the greatest obstacle to your success with the ELS Method, which manifests differently in each step of the process (most commonly by not following the instructions); caused by normal resistance to the greater levels of success and happiness that the process brings when you follow the instructions.

REACTION RESPONSE: when you intentionally create patterns of behavior *in reaction* to what your parents modeled.

RESPONSE LETTER: part of the ELS Letters process, in which you'll receive the *ideal* response from your *ideal* version of the person with whom you're completing ELS Letters; created directly by converting your typed-up Expression Letter line-by-line, according to the instructions in chapter 5.

ROOT EXPERIENCE: the earlier life experience that lays underneath, and gives rise to, your Greatest Current Challenge.

STORY CORE: a positive, empowering memory that is very dear to your heart; sets the vibrational tone of your new story, and everything else will be organized around it.

THE EXPAND AND DISTILL TECHNIQUE: a way to distill Trouble Spots, which involves writing *more* about the Trouble Spot, describing it in *greater* detail, until you experience a breakthrough in your awareness (which may involve a hidden Old Message) that dissolves your confusion.

TROUBLE SPOT: any part of your ELS that feels heavy, confusing, or excessively long, and that is difficult to clarify and pare down; a way to hide the truth, and so they hold breakthroughs inside of them that will be revealed to you, once distilled.

An Invitation

If you're interested in private coaching to optimize your ELS Journey, or in traveling to Achuar territory in the Amazon rainforest with me to connect more deeply to your dreams, please contact me at: www.TheEvolvingArtist.com.

CPSIA information can be obtained
at www.ICGtesting.com
Printed in the USA
LVHW092319100320
649700LV00001B/8/J